Dana

Many Blessings.
Lisa McKee
3/25/2021

CAPACITY

WOMEN SHATTERING THE LIMITS — NOW!

DR. LISA LINDSAY WICKER

ARCHWAY
PUBLISHING

Archway Publishing books may be ordered through booksellers or by contacting:

Archway Publishing
1663 Liberty Drive
Bloomington, IN 47403
www.archwaypublishing.com
844-669-3957

Cover Design: LaTanya Orr
Cover Photographer: Santanna Hayes
Editors: Dr. Mintzi Schramm
Linda Anger
Interior Book Design: Candice T. Holt

ISBN: 978-1-6657-0145-7 (sc)
ISBN: 978-1-6657-0143-3 (hc)
ISBN: 978-1-6657-0144-0 (e)

Library of Congress Control Number: 2021900355

Print information available on the last page.

Archway Publishing rev. date: 02/19/2021

Bestselling author of **The Winning Spirit** and Founder of **Career Mastered**

DR. LISA LINDSAY WICKER

CAPACITY

WOMEN SHATTERING THE LIMITS - NOW!

Foreword by **Florine Mark**, President and CEO of The WW (Weight Watchers) Group, Inc.

ACCOLADES

for

Capacity: Women Shattering
The Limits — Now!

Dr. Lisa Wicker has spoken. "Now" is the time for women to claim their seat at the table and use our Capacity to the fullest. She addresses the difference between Capacity and potential. In the game of business, you've got to know the formula for getting ahead. In *Capacity: Women Shattering The Limits — Now!* Dr. Wicker gives you the 7 steps for women to move forward faster. No matter your career destination, you will benefit from the wisdom and strategies shared by Dr. Wicker. The book is a motivator and call to action for the high-achieving woman who cares about her impact and leadership. I highly recommend you pick up your copy today.

Denise Brooks-Williams
FACHE Senior Vice President
Chief Executive Officer
North Market (SEM-North) Henry Ford Health System

Dr. Wicker's tools and materials have transformed so many lives and occupations. Dr. Wicker is able to put into words some of the things that are hard to express, but you know, simply make sense in business. Her toolbox has helped so many careers, and I am sure it will help many more. This book is a must-read.

David W. Johnson
Owner
Private Asset Management Group

Dr. Lisa Wicker is an incredible leader who has used her considerable industry experience and knowledge in identifying the best talent, helping them flourish, building productive teams, and creating a culture and expectation that made her organizations better. She is considered one of the best in her field and is always willing to share best practices and offer support to those of us who had the pleasure of knowing and working with her around the world. This book, *Capacity: Women Shattering The Limits — Now!* is a must-read if you are serious about owning your Career and Life's Work.

Gary K. Dent
Managing Member
Devine Talent Management, LLC

The moment is now for women to discover and acknowledge the best, authentic version of themselves — and believe it. With this truth, women can crash through the artificial limitations they and other people impose on them. Dr. Wicker's amazing book reveals the mysteries that have held women, prisoners, for so long. With down-to-earth insights and tools, she gives them steps to shatter the myths that have kept them captive and help them discover the path to their truest self. Phenomenal breakthroughs and doable action plans.

Sidney R. Bonvallet, MA, MS
President
Helping Hands Touching Hearts Charity

Dr. Lisa Wicker, recognized as one of "America's Top 100 Executives," is a highly sought after thought leader. In her book, *Capacity: Women Shattering The Limits — Now!* she shares her years of practical experience, wisdom, and insights. Dr. Lisa provides a methodical process to help you, the reader, breakthrough barriers to master your career and your life.

Joan Higginbotham
Retired NASA Astronaut

Look, we all know that women expect they will encounter very real barriers as they advance in their professional careers — we've encountered them ourselves. The real need is for practical approaches to address these barriers so that women can shatter the limits placed before them. Based on Dr. Wicker's own experience and lessons from the hundreds of women she's helped, this book is an invaluable resource!

Jennifer Martineau, PhD
President and Founder
Leap & Inspire Global LLC
Former SVP, Center for Creative Leadership

Caution: the following content is habit-forming. Proceed if you are ready to declare war on "playing small" and are tired of justifying ineffective habits. By activating Dr. Wicker's 7-Step C Framework and clarifying my brand story, I attracted a corporate sponsor, solidified strategic partnerships, and started a new Brand Ambassador role across my social channels. Make reading and re-reading her manual for mastering Capacity a part of your daily routine.

Tisha "The Small Business Cheerleader" Hammond
International best-selling author
Host at 'Pep talk with Tisha Hammond'
Powered by Dell Technologies and Intel Corporation

I have known and worked with Dr. Wicker for over 15 years. Her experience, passion, intelligence, deep understanding of people, and her limitless energy in this field make her uniquely qualified to write this book. She lives an unstoppable life, constantly reducing barriers to speed bumps. Women that aspire to the same should take the time to read her new book, *Capacity: Women Shattering The Limits — Now!*

Simon Boag
Managing Partner
IncWell

Dr. Lisa Wicker is a strong leader, capable of inspiring and mentoring without realizing she is making an impact. She uses her experiences to motivate in productive and positive ways. Through demonstration, she teaches one how to pivot and keep going to achieve outcomes when obstacles surface. She accomplishes this through actions and visibility. Her book, *Capacity: Women Shattering The Limits — Now!* will no doubt provide meaningful insights, teaching nuggets, and roadmaps to shatter limits and achieve desired results.

Marie R. McLucas CPA, CMA
Chief Financial Officer
Primax Properties, LLC

Dr. Lisa Wicker is relentless in helping women have the career and life they want. She is like the big sister who has been there, done that, and wants to help you navigate with fewer hurdles. Even with hurdles, Lisa knows how to break situations down so that you can overcome just about anything. After reading this book, *Capacity: Women Shattering The Limits — Now!* you will be empowered to take your career to the next level, feeling loved, encouraged, and supported.

Dawn Johnson
Owner/Agent
State Farm Insurance

Get ready to be inspired! *Capacity: Women Shattering The Limits — Now!* is a truth-telling, myth-removing powerhouse of a book. Dr. Wicker is an example of leadership in action and life without limits. She shares a 7-Step C framework to help women who are ready to shatter their limits now. The steps are easy to apply, anchored by anecdotes and her leadership experience and reinforced by exercises that keep you focused on your goals. The book is an eye-opener and a life-changer.

Sheri Hunter
Author
Daring to Live

DEDICATION

To all the people who have helped me shatter limits and continue using every ounce of Capacity God gives me:

My family who reared me: John and Johnnie Gardner Sr., LaVerne Gardner Lindsay Stewart, Carolyn Gardner Moore, and my extended family.

My mentors — both women and men, my circle of strong women who always lift me up and my wonderful, dedicated, and talented team.

To the loves of my life:

Justin, Jonathan, Jonas, Analiyah and Jeremiah are my heartbeats. To Michael, my love and best friend who always has my best interest at heart on life's journey.

ACKNOWLEDGEMENTS

This book would not have been possible without the support and love of many people.

I am my mother's daughter. The late LaVerne Gardner Lindsay Stewart was a woman of great insight who always gave me and my siblings protection, hope, values, love and the support to become all we could imagine and more. Without her unconditional love, guidance and nurturing and the strong example of courage and perseverance she provided, I would not be who I am today.

My husband, Michael, my love, my partner of 40 years and the best father and grandfather to our sons and grandchildren, has been the best life partner that God could have provided. Our story is one of many adventures that God has made possible.

My siblings, Dr. Tamara Lindsay Roberts, Louie Lindsay Jr., Teri Lindsay Fobbs and Brenda Lindsay Estes deserve my thanks for being a shining example to me. As the youngest of the family, I eagerly watched each of you and followed in your footsteps. You set the bar for me, and I had no choice but to meet it. I love when we all get together to recall the best of the old days of our growing up in Mississippi. What could have been bleak became a cherished memory. We are so blessed to have been reared by the community and the family that loved us and ensured our success.

Part of my Culture Story is about my community. I would not be able to function successfully without all of those who helped bring this book to life, including my editors, Linda Anger and Dr. Mintzi Schramm. Linda and I met in 2000 and have not let go of one another since that time. She is one of the coolest and smartest people I know. She has been the editor of all three of my books. I am forever grateful to her. Dr. Schramm and I connected many years ago, mainly when I was working on my doctorate. She, too, is one of the best editors I know.

I also want to thank LaTanya, but where do I begin? LaTanya and I met around 1996 at church. We instantly connected, and here we are in 2021, still going strong. Anyone who knows me well knows that LaTanya has been by my side from the very beginning of my entrepreneurial days. She has been my branding guru and the little sister I never had. LaTanya, thank you for loving and supporting me.

A special thanks to all the fantastic people who helped to bring this book to life in so many other ways: Simon Boag, Dr. Jennifer Martineau, Gary Dent, Marie McLucas, David Johnson, Denise Brooks-Williams, Joan Higginbotham, Sheri Hunter, Dawn Johnson, and Candice Holt.

Thank you as well to all the amazing women who have been there for me on many occasions, whether to listen, hug, laugh, scream or cry. You have helped me shatter many limits and supported me to use all my Capacity and grow into the woman I am today.

Sidney Bonvallet, thank you for being a mentor, friend and soulmate, whom I adore and love. Florine Mark, you have shown me by example what women supporting women looks like. You're amazing. Karen Sanford, your friendship and love is esteemed in so many ways. Tisha Hammond, you are the best encourager that I've met in recent years, and your joy is contagious.

To my incredible team at Linwick & Associates, *Career Mastered* Magazine and Excel Village, it's a joy to work side by side with each of you. Thank you for helping me grow my Capacity every day and allow me to give love, guidance, hope and a torch for the next generation of leaders.

FOREWORD

Living life without limits is a choice! Consider my story, in which I chose to design life without limits.

Growing up on the northwest side of Detroit, my nickname in elementary school was "FF," which stood for "Fat Flo." When I was 12, I started taking a mix of amphetamines, thyroid pills, and tranquilizers to curb my appetite. At 16, I got married, lost weight to fit into my wedding dress, but gained it all back a few months later. By the time I was 25 and the mother of five children, my size 22 was causing health problems. I didn't believe in myself. But, instead of solely focusing on my weight loss, I decided to help others with theirs.

I first discovered Weight Watchers in the 1960s when I saw an ad for the studio while flipping through a *Woman's Day* magazine. When I called the number listed, I was told there were no locations in Michigan. So, I left my five children with my parents and husband and took off for Queens, New York, where I attended a week's worth of classes and meetings in the home of Weight Watchers founder Jean Nidetch.

Within one week of following Weight Watcher's points-based, healthy-eating system, I lost five pounds. After four months, I had dropped 40. I influenced Nidetch to bring a studio to Michigan, and she agreed.

Getting a loan to build it proved more challenging. Armed with a business plan and sales projections, I went to the local bank and applied for a $5,000 loan — but the bank would only grant it if my husband signed as CEO and president. I told them he wouldn't be signing since I was the CEO and owner. They denied me the loan.

"Shattering Limits," I eventually found a bank willing to lend the money and debuted my first studio in Detroit. I never felt that there was a glass ceiling and truly believed that not anything or anyone could stop me.

I expanded Weight Watchers to the Midwest, Canada and Mexico. Weight Watchers sparked a weight-loss movement in the 1970s and 1980s. Eventually, I became a national face of the brand and the world's largest franchisee of Weight Watchers studios, at one point owning locations in 14 states and three countries.

Dr. Wicker and I have been blessed beyond all expectations. Yet, I think our greatest shared blessing is that we both have been able — through our respective platforms — to teach and inspire others to shatter limitations while striving to reach their purposes.

Capacity: Women Shattering The Limits — Now! is a book about women being true to themselves at every stage of the journey so they can use every ounce of their Capacity to live life to the fullest. This book offers reality-based plans for those seeking to make their future even more productive. Dr. Wicker provides the reader with a blend of practical and pragmatic steps to reach their dreams. The 7-Step C framework included herein identifies and articulates an approach that can help women break free now to pursue exciting opportunities. We both encourage you to refuse to accept limitations — imposed by others or those you place on yourself.

I am confident that the thinking found within this book will enable many more women to move from concept to a plan to master their careers and life without limits. Now, your best is yet to come.

Florine Mark
President and CEO
The WW (Weight Watchers) Group, Inc.

CAPACITY

ca·pac·i·ty

1. The facility or power to produce, perform or deploy

2. The power or ability to do it now

TABLE OF CONTENTS

Part One

OVERVIEW

My Vision

I made the choice to not blame my circumstances but
to be true to myself at every stage of the journey.
Lisa Lindsay Wicker

I have the vision to advance women's leadership, and I work on this vision each day. I imagine that women will use their Capacity to shatter old rules, refuse to accept limitations imposed by others or those they place on themselves, set their measure of success and design the life and career of their dreams. Ultimately, gender-equality would be a nonissue, and women and men would see leadership in a new and limitless way to share power at the top. Lastly, I imagine that women will adopt the practices outlined in *Capacity: Women Shattering The Limits — Now!*

In more than 30 years of working with women in business, I have encountered many who have achieved a remarkable degree of success. I have also found many struggling with a deep need and thirst to find their voice and move past perceived limits to live the life of their dreams.

I am sure some of the problems shared with me about what holds them back are familiar to you:

1. I'm an excessive planner, and I overthink everything. I was meant to be an entrepreneur; yet, I'm working a job every day to make someone else wealthy. Why am I afraid to step into my calling?

2. I love my employees and believe that I provide the right work environment. While they're loyal, I don't trust them enough to delegate essential matters and find myself burned out.

3. I've attempted to set up meetings with others I think would be great mentors and whom I would like in my circle. I didn't get a response. It's frustrating to be ghosted.

4. Because of past failures on the job, I struggle with finding an answer as to why my superiors or colleagues don't respect me. I feel that I'm stuck and am unsure how to move forward without self-doubt.

5. I find that my tactics and gifts are hidden in my current job; yet, I must continue working because I have bills to pay. Unless I see something different soon, I'm stuck here, wasting away.

6. I need to be better at time management. At the end of my day, I often stop and reflect on where I spent my time. I'm busy being busy and don't feel that I'm living my best life.

7. I've worked just as hard and better than my white male colleague; yet, he got the promotion, not based upon merit. I feel invisible.

8. I'm good at what I do at work. I'm incredibly comfortable leading my team; yet, I don't feel I've found my voice to make an impact in this world.

Many women relate to pain points such as betrayal, anger, hurt, powerlessness, settling for mediocre, feeling defeated or depressed and just plain stuck. They're real. Like many of the women I've coached, mentored and supported, I've faced problems and challenges on my way to the executive suite. I even felt that what was happening to me in certain employment situations was not fair or unjust. At times, I felt helpless.

Still, I learned early on that I needed to help myself. Starting my career in the male-dominated automotive manufacturing environment at the age of 21, I quickly learned that no one else would step in if I didn't step up and fight for myself. I decided not to blame my circumstances but to be true to myself at every stage of the journey and to use every ounce of Capacity on and off the job. After 30-plus years in corporate hallways, I left to begin my next chapter. I decided to help other women succeed. From the time I started my professional career in the early 80s, I had high hopes that women would have made much further progress than we have achieved to date.

Women today lead 167 of the country's top 3,000 companies. That's more than double that of a decade ago, but still under 6%. For many, the barrier isn't just the glass ceiling at the very top but also an invisible wall that sidelines them from the kind of roles that have been traditional steppingstones to the CEO position.[1]

It's remarkable that during this day and age, when more women are taking over power positions, poor representation in business and gender equity continues to be the norm. Studies indicate that women are underrepresented in corporations, and the share of women decreases with each step up the corporate hierarchy. Women encounter many real barriers to advancement into leadership positions, including gender discrimination and unconscious gender bias. A study by McKinsey and Company confirmed that invisible walls are holding women back, rather than overt sexism alone.[2] Although proven bad for business, these realities continue to exist. Data further shows that increasingly women don't receive near as much investment capital as their male counterparts.

The McKinsey study also found that if every country could narrow its gender gap at the same historical rate as the fastest improving nation in its regional peer group, the world could add $12 trillion to its annual gross domestic product by 2025.[3] Just think about that!

There are proven benefits that women bring to organizations and the marketplace. The data suggest that the deck is stacked against women on the road to business success, whether working to realize their first big idea or to secure the corner office.

At the beginning of 2020, women's representation in corporate America was trending in the right direction. This was most pronounced in senior management: Between January 2015 and January 2020, representation of women in senior-vice-president positions grew from 23 to 28 percent, and representation in the C-suite rose from 17 to 21 percent.

Women — particularly women of color — remained dramatically under-represented, but the numbers were slowly improving.[4] The Covid-19 pandemic pressures are driving some employees — especially women — to consider downshifting their careers or leaving the workforce. It's predicted that the Covid-19 crisis could set women back a decade.[5]

Regardless of the proven benefits women leaders bring to the marketplace, the challenges remain, and we're actively participating in the game by accepting some of these illusions. I know because, for a while, I believed them myself.

In my leadership development programs, I encourage women to take back their power, permit themselves to win, develop their voice, be true to themselves and get clear about their career vision.

Well, I will say it: You would think that we wouldn't continue down the same path when it's leading nowhere. You would think we would take a different route, choose differently. But that's not always the case. I, however, am interested in you creating a clear strategy for winning by using your Capacity to break free of any limits and to design the career and life you desire. Whatever winning means for you — a new job, a new partner, a profitable business, work from anywhere and anytime — you need a framework, a strategy to make it happen.

Over the years, I've had the privilege of designing winning strategies for thousands of people from all over the world. I want to meet you where you are and help you face your fears. The goal is to erase self-doubts, to clarify your purpose and determine what you are uniquely designed to create in this world. In short, I want to help you find your voice and message and engineer your path to success. To do that, you need to connect your Culture Story from intent to impact so that you walk in alignment with fulfilling opportunities.

My success is based upon shattering limits and using every ounce of Capacity I own — and then some. It's also based on these Three Golden Rules of Success:

1. NAME IT BEFORE YOU CLAIM IT

For me, there's no denying that God created everything with words. By the same token, you're designed to create your success with your words. When you say you're going to do something, commit to it. That's how you create with words. You say you're going to do this thing. Then, you have to commit to it and act on it to get the results to claim it. Then, move on to the next thing. Use your words to say what you're going to do and make it happen. You have everything you need to name it and claim it.

2. WALK BEFORE YOU RUN

This book started with my words, which I claimed according to my first golden rule of success. I began to walk toward what I named while mastering each step of the walk. For example, when I began to take dance lessons, I walked until, eventually, I was ready to run at clip speed by participating in a local Dancing with the Stars. So, I believe we must be willing to walk before we can run. Even as you are reading this book, I want you to engage, to complete each "take action" assignment and all the work required. You must walk before you can run. You must name it before you can claim it.

3. TAKE CONSISTENT ACTION BECAUSE LIFE REWARDS ACTION

People don't care about our intentions and empty words. Intentions are only meaningful when you turn them into action. People care about what we do. My goal is not to help you develop a list of intentions that never become results. My goal is to help you create the purposeful action necessary to bring forth the results you desire. Every moment in which we fail to take purposeful action is another moment wasted.

Here's how these Three Golden Rules of Success have helped me on my journey:

Like you, I've had many moments of not being sure and even not being ready. Even recently, was not quite ready to launch the *Career Mastered* Magazine. Yet, I had named it. I was ready to claim it, and in 2015 I took the first steps to that dream.

After launching the Career Mastered Awards program in 2015, I decided it would be great to get media coverage on the remarkable women we had honored across the United States.

I reached out to several major magazines, and of course, most were not willing to feature our honorees. If they did, it was on their terms, with imposed limits. So, I said, "I don't need permission to achieve the desired results that I have envisioned." What do you know — less than three months later, the *Career Mastered* Magazine was conceived, designed, written, printed and launched with significant support.

MY POINT

I did everything you're going to learn in this book. I named it before I claimed it (I created the magazine with my words).

I walked before I ran (running at clip speed).

I took consistent action because life rewards action.

The results came and continue to come! The magazine launched with hundreds of people attending welcome parties in New York, Detroit and Charlotte.

I want you to create those moments for yourself. Please do it by remembering my 3 Golden Rules of Success:

1. Name it before you claim it! You can create anything with your words. Claim it.

2. Walk Before You Run! Complete every action step in this book, and commit to the process. Before you know it, you'll be running your race.

3. Take Consistent Action because life rewards action. Say what you want, take action on it, commit to it!

I CAN'T WAIT TO SEE YOUR RESULTS!

7-Step C Framework

From now on!
Lisa Lindsay Wicker

*C*apacity: Women Shattering The Limits — Now! is a culmination of what I've learned over the past three decades of my corporate career and entrepreneurial journey. Both as a corporate executive and an entrepreneur, I've spent countless hours coaching and guiding women on removing limits, whether imposed by others or themselves. This book is for high-achieving women who are ready to use their Capacity and shatter any limits to create their desired future. It offers reality-based plans for those seeking to make their future even more productive.

In these pages, I'll share the backbone of this book — my 7-Step C Framework that expands your Capacity so you can pursue exciting opportunities and design the career and life of your dreams. Understanding you and helping you focus your efforts in harmony with your goals is the spirit of this book. The steps are easy to apply, anchored by anecdotes based upon my leadership experience and reinforced by exercises that keep you focused on your goals. You'll find wisdom and practical advice to be central. You'll discover why the time is now to shatter the limits, and you'll learn the following:

* How to clarify your purpose in record time to determine what you're uniquely designed to create in this world.

- How to connect your Culture Story from intent to impact, so you walk in alignment and flow into momentum to manifest your point of view and attract new and fulfilling opportunities.

- How to create your authentic brand content that reflects what you've been called to communicate to this world.

- How to face your fears, conquer limiting beliefs and self-doubt so that you create with confidence and power to access your dream life.

- How to move from concept to a viable 7-Step Action Plan to master your career and life, without limits.

This book is also made available to participants in my Shatter the Limits Masterclass. I advise them to see the book as a growth companion. It's organized incrementally with suggestions for immediate application. If you're like me, you can be a bit of a know-it-all and decide to skip around. While this book's advice is not rocket science, each step is dependent on the other, sequentially. My recommendation is to follow the sequence. That way you'll get the most out of the applications.

The next page is a visual representation of the sequence and the integration of the 7-Step C Framework to acquiring your dreams. It will be used to explore the sequential relationship between the steps, various methodologies and how they relate to each other. Each of the concepts will be explained and will be highlighted as it's introduced. Remember that completing each milestone takes you one step closer to your desired goal. Follow the Motivational Milestone Map at the end of each section. It will guide you through the steps and provide a line of sight on your progress.

One of my mentors told me that a successful acceleration strategy needs to start from the foundation of what the critical player thinks possible. Sometimes it's necessary to diagnose readiness. So, I ask you to take a moment to diagnose your readiness to follow the 7-Step C Framework to shatter the limits and create your future. If you're ready, your time is *Now*! The future you has already arrived. Let's go!

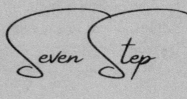

Seven Step

"C" FRAMEWORK

Culture
Story
Clarity
Consistency
Commitment
Capacity
Conquer
Convert

Part Two

THE FUNDAMENTALS

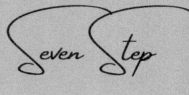

"C" FRAMEWORK

Culture
Story

Clarity

Consistency

Commitment

Capacity

Conquer

Convert

Culture Story:

WHO AM I?

Milestone One

Your Culture Story
The Bridge to Your Destiny

Your story is what you have, what you will always have.
It's something to own.
Michelle Obama

You're smart, engaged, strong and driven to accomplish something meaningful. As a high-achieving woman, you know there's more — that's why you're continually searching for the next advantage to propel your quantum leap over the latest imposed limits of your career.

So, what do you want? What's your value add? The answer to this question is your Culture Story. This is the bridge to your destiny.

Culture Story is an important term because where we come from has such a strong effect on the person we've become. I believe your culture is an important part of who you are.

Like personality, culture consists of the values, beliefs, underlying assumptions, interests, experiences, upbringing and habits that create behavior. We women are often so busy managing, directing, leading, setting and achieving goals that we forget to ask the question, Who am I? To become all that we are intended to be, we must cultivate self-awareness.

Did you know that your Culture Story has value? It's made you strong. Yet, sometimes we ignore its value because some parts of the story may need to be rewritten. The key is to find the value-add in your Culture Story so you can confidently take the necessary steps to create your brand messages and present your authority in line with your goals and purpose.

In my research and coaching on career transitions, I've observed many women who know they want to make a change but struggle to articulate what they want to do next. I've also observed and coached women who have effectively mastered the ability to achieve their goals, gain support systems and become a brand authority in their specific area of influence. The difference is the ability to own and share the narrative of a compelling Culture Story in the pursuit of purpose.

WHY YOUR CULTURE STORY MAKES A DIFFERENCE

Culture Stories define us. It's so easy to underestimate the value of sharing yours. A compelling Culture Story inspires others to believe in you, your value, your character and your ability to be an authority and agency of your brand.

Each day whether you're consciously aware of it or not, you're selling your brand. Only you can provide an effective narrative about who you are, your identity, strengths, interest, failures, value add and everything in between. No one else can be authentically you. Your Culture Story is the most powerful part of who you are. It connects to universal truths.

In my consulting practice, I teach women how to own their Culture Story. Many of my clients find this activity somewhat challenging and a bit raw because most of us don't take the time to look inward and to ask the question, Who Am I? Uncovering your voice means going through this process to confidently define who you are so that you can position yourself to provide a compelling value proposition in every situation. When you're in transition, feeling stuck, or have decided that it's time for you to create your dream life or career, your Culture Story will help you release the past and embrace the future.

HOW YOU IDENTIFY SHAPES YOUR CULTURE STORY

Your Culture Story will give you the self-awareness to identify how you add value so that you can own your power. When you know your value, you can create meaning and purpose and become your personal brand authority. Now, I'm not saying you must advertise yourself on YouTube or be on the cover of *Career Mastered* or *Time* magazine. What I am saying is that you advertise yourself every day to those you interact with by how you conduct yourself. Consciously, most of us aren't aware of it; yet, we're always creating a personal brand that influences how others see us. If you don't define yourself, you could easily be inaccurately defined by others. If I were to ask you today, how you describe your brand or explain your brand authority, you should be able to articulate your value proposition or critical point of differentiation.

In today's environment of Instagram, YouTube, Facebook, LinkedIn and social media in general, authority is what makes or breaks the individual. These social media tools have allowed individuals to become instant authorities, especially if they are used to selling themselves as entrepreneurs, coaches, trainers or consultants.

Some high-achieving women have been able to quit their day jobs because of their ability to build their brand authority online

19

and significantly up their game. Many have become game-changers based on the brands they've developed and their ability to market themselves with a message that resonates with the receiver.

Now, don't get me wrong. I know that not all women are looking to become the next big influencer on social media. What I am talking about is taking a lesson from some of these women who have become successful. They've built personal brand power that yields authority — the kind of brand authority and emotional power that opens big doors and leads to new opportunities, connections and business ventures.

I hear some of you saying that's not what I want. Perhaps, you don't — not in the manner of being a social media influencer. Neither do I.

But here's the thing you must understand: Everyone wants personal brand authority — the power to lead in your lane. Sometimes we're just not aware that this type of authority is what we're after.

I recall a meeting with one of my mentors while working at General Motors. We were talking about my goals, and I said:

> Skip, I'm ready for a promotion to the next level. I've done the hard work, I've checked all the boxes I've been asked to check; yet, it hasn't happened. There are too many barriers to my becoming an executive.

He asked me one question:

Why do you want the promotion to the executive role?"

I told him I was ready and prepared for it. He said:

That's not the answer. When you think you have the answer, set up another meeting with me and let's discuss the best next steps toward your goal.

I went home and thought about his question. I came up with several answers and set up the next meeting about a week later. He asked me again:

Why do you want the promotion?

My answer:

I'm a leader, considered high potential, and have the skill-set necessary to perform the job now.

He didn't respond right away. When he did, he said:

A lot of people — including the janitor — are leaders and have the skill-set to get that next promotion. It doesn't matter if you're the CEO or the janitor, you have to know why you want to lead at each level. I'm going to give you the answer so that as you grow in your career you'll understand the why of your desire for growth as a leader. You want to be promoted so that you have the authority to make decisions — and you have something important to give, say and do while influencing others. Authority is what's necessary to help people connect with your point of view.

Skip and I often met even after I was positioned to have authority. What I learned is that authority isn't something that you give to yourself. Authority is bestowed by others, and you get it as part of your career journey, when others acknowledge that you have something important to give, do or say.

Personal brand authority is all about the right people believing in your perspective or way of doing business — whether you're in the room or not.

YOUR BRAND AUTHORITY WILL SPEAK FOR YOU.

Creating a personal brand authority is perhaps one of the critical important elements of your career success strategy. It's your edge — your marketing edge. Just as companies use it for a competitive position in the marketplace, so too must you use it. As we begin the 7-Step C Framework to lift your Capacity, let's take a look at the first steps to focus your efforts in harmony with your goals.

DEVELOP YOUR PERSONAL BRAND
AUTHORITY BIOGRAPHY

Your personal brand authority is your leadership point of view, which equates to your expertise and experience. Your Culture Story is the catalyst for your personal brand authority. Much of your ability to command authority will be based upon the uniqueness of your Culture Story. One of the best ways to differentiate your point of view is to craft your personal brand authority bio, which will serve your ability to set you apart.

The idea behind writing your Culture Story and then developing your personal brand authority bio is to ensure that you are confident in who you are and your power. This confidence must develop before you can build the trust necessary to help people connect with your point of view and command authority in your industry.

The content of this bio is not the same as your typical biography or résumé. So what content is included in your brand authority? Think of it as something to market your point of view — your leadership expertise and experience. Your brand authority bio will begin with your Culture Story identity mapped to your experience content and written in the first person. It's designed to differentiate you while creating awareness. It provides the right content at the right time every time to educate and engage others and thereby convert your dreams into desired outcomes.

CURATE THE RIGHT MOMENTS TO HEIGHTEN YOUR PERSONAL BRAND AUTHORITY

Calling forth your brand authority will eventually become a matter of habit, but it won't start that way. Here's how it works: You're at one of the most coveted business networking events of the year and are introduced to the one person you've hoped to meet for some time. Because you have a plan to integrate your brand authority with your overall brand presence, you're ready to value up and amplify the areas of content needed at that moment. When you're able to sense opportunities and find ways to heighten your brand authority bio while motivating others to share it — you've become an authority figure. The more you use your brand authority as a tool to create opportunities and connections the better you'll get at communicating and networking with its content.

As we work together towards shattering limits and using your Capacity to reach the goals you desire, remember: It all starts with your Culture Story!

TAKE ACTION NOW

When you learn how to use your identity elements to form a narrative, you'll discover your Culture Story, which leads to your personal brand authority bio.

Let's start your Culture Story. It will include:

- Name
- Identity
- Interests
- Accomplishments
- Fascination
- Strengths
- Challenges
- Value propositions
  (What makes you unique, and how you help others)

Next, I'll give you several examples of your story's elements so that you can write your own Culture Story, which will lead to your written personal brand authority bio.

YOUR STORY ELEMENTS

Identity
Your answer to the question: Who am I? is your identity. It can be age, birthplace, socioeconomic status, sexual orientation, gender, etc. Your identity is how you define yourself or how others define you.[1] List your identifiers, Subsequently, select

the top three of this list that could differentiate you in the marketplace. For example:

Identity 1: First African American Female International VP
Identity 2: Born in Mississippi
Identity 3: Publisher, *Career Mastered* Magazine

Often, we give no credence to our identity. Yet, your identity is what draws people and makes them want to learn more about you or choose to build a relationship with you rather than someone else.

Here's my example: I started my career as a summer intern for one of the world's largest automotive organizations. From there I moved on to large retail and entertainment companies. My career trajectory was from a student to a successful executive; in the process, I was recognized as the first African American woman to make this remarkable transition in a particular company.

Guess what? When clients call for consultations, they said they reached out to me precisely because they share the same goals and hope to achieve a similar career.

Strengths

According to Gallup, whether you're looking to become a leader or are already in a leadership position and want to empower your people to perform better, your efforts start with identifying your strengths.[2]

Your strengths contribute a great deal to your Culture Story so it's important to identify them. To do that, reflect on where you demonstrate your strengths. Putting them in context and seeing them in action will help you understand what they are and how these strengths translate to skills.

The following are some sample strengths:

Strength 1: Creative
Strength 2: Great listener
Strength 3: Problem solver
Strength 4: Fashion forward
Strength 5: Relationship builder

Interests

What do you enjoy doing? I love reading self-help books, attending leadership conferences, learning the latest social media networking tips and watching reality shows, such as Survivor and the Real Housewives. Interest is about inquisitiveness: wanting to know or learn about something or someone.[3]

The following are some sample interests:

Interest 1: Reading
Interest2: Attending Conferences
Interest 3: Networking.

Fascination

You're fascinating, and people love it. What you know is sought after. What you've overcome is compelling to people.[4] Your Culture Story should include why people need your help and what they can learn from you. Why do they seek your expertise?

What do your family and friends admire about you? What do people compliment you on? Think back to your conversations this past week. Did you post something on social media that got people's attention? Has anyone private-messaged you, complimented you on something or asked for your praise or feedback?

The following are some examples of fascination others have about you:

Fascination 1: How did you publish a global magazine?
Fascination 2: How did you go from an intern position to being an executive?
Fascination 3: How did you land your dream job?
Fascination 4: How did you start three successful businesses?

Accomplishments

What accomplishments stand out in your life? Typically, accomplishments are wins that we celebrate.[5]

The following are some examples of accomplishments or wins:

Win 1: Children graduated from college
Win 2: Career Mastered Women's History Leadership Award created
Win 3: Dancing with the Stars finalist

Challenges

Challenges are difficult areas where you lack strength or are fragile.[6]

The following are some examples of challenges:

Challenge 1: Loss of both parents.
Challenge 2: Growing up in the segregated south.
Challenge 3: Scaling the business globally.

Now it's time for you to take action to write your own culture story.

Begin with your Culture Story. Reflect on it, and don't be afraid to edit it. You may need more than one draft to capture your truths.

Culture
STORY TEMPLATE

I am _____.

I live in _____.

I am a/an:

A. _____

B. _____

C. _____

My blend of skills have allowed me to:

Accomplishment 1 _____

Accomplishment 2 _____

Accomplishment 3 _____

People inquire often about this part of my life [Sought-after].

Something compelling that people do not know about me [Interests].

Living my best life and my purpose [My Why] is an essential part of my goals.

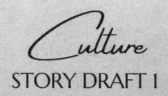

STORY DRAFT 1

I am Dr. Lisa J. Lindsay Wicker. I live in Metropolitan Detroit, MI, and Charlotte, NC. I am a Human Resources Expert and Career Strategist. The secret to my success is positioning myself and understanding what drives me, stops me, and how to meet my expectations and my dreams.

Inquiries from friends, colleagues, clients on where I've been and why: 'How did you ascend from a summer intern to becoming an officer in a major Fortune 50 Corporate America company? How did you succeed in a male-dominated environment? How do you manage to accomplish that which you set out to do? How does your faith help you remain courageous? How did you learn to master your career? Can you help me find my voice to master my career successfully?'

Something compelling that people do not know about me is that I believe in community and find that giving back to others is rewarding. I am the mother of two sons and three grands. I have been married for 40 years.

I'm determined to live my best life. My passion is to support and help other women and girls succeed in creating winning futures. This is what keeps me focused on my goals never to stop learning or growing. Life is learning.

STORY DRAFT 2

I am Dr. Lisa J. Lindsay Wicker. I live in Metropolitan Detroit, MI and Charlotte, NC. I am a Human Resources Expert and Career Strategist. The secret to my success is positioning myself and understanding what drives me, stops me and how to meet my expectations and my dreams.

I have a unique perspective because I was able to move past the separate but equal days of living in the Mississippi Delta in the early 1960s. Because it takes a village to raise a child, my village lifted me. Today, with a dynamic influential approach to life and an iconic signature style, I connect people across the world and find my mission to be that of helping others to get the most out of their work lives by removing limits, and helping companies create value and build capacity. I share my contemporary, relevant work life experiences and empowering principles with my clients as demonstrated in my books, *The Winning Spirit, and Power Play!*

Something compelling that people do not know about me is that I believe in community and find that giving back to others is rewarding. I am the mother of two sons and three grands. I have been married for 40 years. I'm determined to live my best life. My passion is to support and help other women and girls succeed in creating winning futures. This is what keeps me focused on my goals to never stop learning or growing. Life is learning.

Once your Culture Story is written, you'll be able to see who you are, what you stand for and what you want to be. Your Culture Story positions you and gives you the ability to amplify your brand authority.

Only after writing your Culture Story can you write your brand authority bio. This biography will include your message describing what you do, whom you do it for and why you're the best person for the job. To master your career and life, you'll need to communicate why people should work with you or why you're the one for the job.

Let's look at what I've included in my bio, taking the information I developed from my Culture Story:

1. The expertise I provide and why it matters. By including this, clients, potential customers, employers and others can easily imagine working with me.

2. Results I've demonstrated and why. For example, when I work with people, what do they accomplish?

3. Whom do I help? The most influential brands narrow their focus to a targeted audience.

4. What makes me different or uniquely qualified — more than my competition?

Your Culture Story makes you different, and no one else can own it. Your identity, strengths and skills show that you're qualified to be the authority in a specific space.

BRAND AUTHORITY BIOGRAPHY

Now combine your Culture Story and the answers to the above questions into your personal brand authority bio.

Hi, I am Dr. Lisa Lindsay Wicker, an accomplished, award-winning, internationally recognized thought leader, human resources expert, and career strategist. The secret to my success and what I believe is key to positioning myself is to know what drives me, know what stops me, know how to meet my expectations and dreams! And when I dream, dream in great detail, write the vision, and from time to time, allow others to edit it. Respected as a credible voice in decision making, finding strategic business and investment partners while establishing governance boundaries and harnessing the power of community, I earn a seat at the table wherever I serve.

This is not by accident. It is part of my story. You see, I was born in the Mississippi Delta, and I understand the value of my southern roots and the community that rallied around one another in the 1960s to ensure success. I learned early on that my purse is not my worth and that human capital is golden. I was taught that giving up is not an option, and detours are planned in advance for repairs and maintenance needs that arise in working with trained, qualified and reliable teams.

With a dynamic influential approach to life and an iconic signature style, I connect people across the world and find my mission to be that of helping others to get the most out of their work lives by removing limits, and companies to create value and build capacity. I share my contemporary relevant work life experiences and empowering principles with my clients as demonstrated in my books, *The Winning Spirit, and Power Play!*

Following prominent human resources careers with Fortune 50 Companies, I established my Detroit, MI and Charlotte, NC firm, Linwick & Associates, LLC (LWA). LWA is a global human resources firm dedicated to creating organizational value through people. With more than 30 years experience creating organizational value and business results through people, I have earned the reputation as a sought-after expert in the field of HR, change management, learning, DEI, and career development. With my exposure to leaders within business communities across Corporate America and far beyond our borders, I have inspired women to gain confidence to climb the ladder so many find themselves stuck on.

Keeping "community" top of mind is how I have maximized my output and created the classic, iconic and powerful brand called Career Mastered, a leadership network to advance today's global career woman.

To sum it up, I am an entrepreneur, author, speaker, wife, mother and friend whose passion is to help professional women break free to intentionally design and create a future not based on the past, so they can master their careers and life without limits.

It's the reason my new book released this year, called, *Capacity: Women Shattering the Limits—Now!* I am beyond thrilled to share my experiences, expertise with high-achieving women who are ready to move forward, Now!

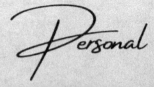

BRAND AUTHORITY BIOGRAPHY

Take Action Now: Write Your Personal Brand Authority
Biography (written in the first person)

_____
_____
_____
_____
_____
_____
_____
_____
_____
_____
_____
_____
_____
_____
_____
_____
_____
_____
_____
_____
_____
_____
_____
_____

Motivational Milestone Map

Specific Measurable Results to Deliver Each Week

M | ap the ideas and concepts.
A | ct on initiatives.
P | rogress to results — to your next level dream.

Week 1   Week 2   Week 3   Week 4   Week 5   Week 6

Culture Story
Masterpiece
Personal Brand
Authority Bio

MILESTONE ONE
Executive Summary

1. As a high-achieving woman, you know there's more. That's why you're continually searching for the next opportunity to boost your quantum leap over your career's latest imposed limits.

2. Your Culture Story will give you the self-awareness to identify how you add value. When you know your worth, you can create meaning and purpose and become your own brand authority to make listeners or readers lean forward to want to know more about you.

3. An effective narrative about who you are includes: your identity, strengths, interest, failures, value add and everything in between. Your Culture Story is the most powerful part of who you are.

4. Your Culture Story is the catalyst for your brand authority, which equates to your leadership expertise and experience. This is what sets you apart.

5. When you're in transition, when you're feeling stuck or when you've finally decided that it's time for you to create your dream life or career, your Culture Story will help you release the past and embrace the future.

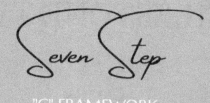

"C" FRAMEWORK

Culture
Story

Clarity

Consistency

Commitment

Capacity

Conquer

Convert

 : COHERENT
PRECISE
TRANSPARENT
EASILY UNDERSTOOD

MILESTONE TWO

Clarity
Getting Clear on Your Target

The best way to predict your future is to create it.
Abraham Lincoln

When you realize that your Culture Story matters, chances are that others will too. Sharing your story allows you to embrace it; that includes your experiences and your truths. These truths enable you to clarify what you have to offer the world. They also spell out for you what your goals are; in other words, the answers to: What do I want? What must I do to have it? How will I feel when I have it? Whom am I helping?

To answer these questions, you must have clarity. Clarity is defined as being coherent, precise, transparent and easily understood. When you know your targeted goals, there is no room for confusion about what's desired. When we're unsure about the targeted goals, we become confused and distracted.

Take Jennifer Smith, who was frustrated with her role as a senior accountant at a Big Four accounting firm. She was clear on one thing: She wasn't happy in her job and wanted a chance to find her voice. She was unsure which path she should take because she loved working with foster care children and always wanted to start her own nonprofit organization. She also felt that her side hustle tax service was where she should focus more of her time because she was appreciated in this role. She felt rewarded doing taxes for the underserved and frustrated with her day job. She knew that she needed to be clear on her targeted goals. As we worked together, Jennifer became clear that she first needed to identify her Culture Story: her strengths, accomplishments, challenges, interests and fascinations. This step would give her clarity on what she could offer the world. Jennifer's Culture Story provided her with the self-awareness to identify how she adds value. As a result, she became clear on her targeted goals.

When you know your value, you can create meaning and purpose and become your brand authority to make listeners lean forward to learn more about you.

ARE YOU MAJORING IN MINOR THINGS?

Step 2 of the 7-Step C Framework is about identifying your targeted goals so you can use your Capacity to shatter limits and create the future you desire. Goals must be expressed in terms of specific events and behaviors.

Ask yourself, do you major in minor things? Jennifer and I decided that she would work on major things rather than minor things and that she would prefer an elephant hunt rather than an ant hunt. Being an elephant identifier would keep her laser-focused on things that are high priority.

The way to determine the right elephant for you to hunt is to apply the 80/20 principle — also known as the Pareto Principle — which states that approximately 20 percent of what you do yields 80 percent of the results, and conversely, 80 percent of what you do yields 20 percent of the results.[1]

Vilfredo Pareto, an Italian economist, first described this principle after observing that 20 percent of the people in Italy owned 80 percent of the wealth. During my retail career, I found that 20 percent of the customers made 80 percent of the complaints. Another way to look at this principle is that 20 percent of your to-do list yields 80 percent of the value. Learn to concentrate most of your time on these items. Finish the others as quickly as possible with the minimum time required.

When setting goals, the idea is to make elephant hunting your highest priority. There will always be elephants and ants in our lives. Unfortunately, we tend to go after ants rather than elephants because they provide a quick kill and a higher body count. But remember, killing ants doesn't put much meat on the table. Hunting elephants does.

A PROMISE STATEMENT IS A GUIDING PURPOSE

When talking to clients, I often learn that some women don't set goals because:

- They don't think they can attain them.
- They think they don't know how.
- They have a fear of failing.
- They don't want to change their pattern of living even though they say they do.

The bottom line is that goals should be things you want to do, and they don't have to be hard to accomplish. They must be specific, measurable, achievable, relevant and time-bound (SMART).[2]

I asked Jennifer to review her Culture Story to understand where she added value. For her to be clear on her targeted goals and achieve them, she would then need to take these steps:

- Decide what you want.
- Decide what price you're willing to pay.
- Write the specifics of your goals.
- Write dates for accomplishing your goals.
- Develop a detailed, scheduled plan of action.
- Determine how you make a difference.
- Decide what you're passionate about.
- Determine what gives you rich satisfaction.
- Determine what you stand for — your Why.

I asked Jennifer to look in the mirror and be honest with herself about why she thought now was the time to find her voice and her purpose. Then she was to list her five most significant priorities in life. With this information and an awareness of her priorities, she would develop her promise to herself about how she would show up in the world. To establish her Big Promise Goal statement, she would start with the end in mind considering themes from her Culture Story, including the following points:

- Who are you?
- What have you accomplished?
- Who have you helped and why is it important for you to help them?

- Can you monetize this promise goal?
- Does it allow you to use your brand authority?

This promise goal would be the elephant target that would give her life meaning and purpose. It would be her guiding purpose, and how she would show up in the world. Writing down her Big Promise Goal as a statement would be part of the strategy to get her from point A to point Z.

LET'S TAKE ACTION NOW

To get clear on your guiding purpose, write your Big Promise Goal using the template provided.

PROMISE GOAL
MY GUIDING PURPOSE

I help_____

to_____

so that they can _____

_____

_____

_____

_____.

My goal is to:

_____

_____

_____

_____

_____

by_____.

Big

PROMISE GOAL
MY GUIDING PURPOSE
(SAMPLE)

I help high achieving women break free to intentionally design and create a future not based on the past, so that they can master their careers and life without limits. My goal is to launch a masterclass by September 2020 that will have a global impact to advance women's leadership.

Motivational
Milestone Map

Specific Measurable Results to Deliver Each Week

M | ap the ideas and concepts.
A | ct on initiatives.
P | rogress to results — to your next level dream.

Week 1   Week 2   Week 3   Week 4   Week 5   Week 6

Culture Story   Big Promise
Masterpiece   Goal
Personal
Brand
Authority Bio

MILESTONE TWO
Executive Summary

1. Your truth allows you to become clear on what you have to offer the world. It defines your goals and answers the questions: What do I want? What must I do to get it? How will I feel when I get it? Whom am I helping?

2. The way to determine the right elephant for you to hunt is to apply the 80/20 principle: 20 percent of what you do yields 80 percent of the results, and conversely, 80 percent of what you do yields 20 percent of the results.

3. When setting goals, make elephant hunting your highest priority.

4. The bottom line is that goals should be something you want to do, and they don't have to be hard to achieve. They must be specific, measurable, achievable, relevant and time-bound (SMART).

5. The Big Promise Goal is the elephant target that would give your life meaning and purpose. This promise goal should become your guiding purpose.

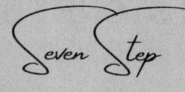

"C" FRAMEWORK

Culture
Story

Clarity

Consistency

Commitment

Capacity

Conquer

Convert

Consistency

STEADFAST
ADHERENCE IN THE APPLICATION OF SOMETHING
RELIABLE OR UNIFORMITY OF SUCCESSIVE RESULTS

MILESTONE THREE

Consistency
Life Rewards Action

We become what we want to be
by consistently being what we want to become each day.
Richard G. Scott

T o be consistent is a commitment we make either to ourselves or sometimes to others. It's about a promise to carry out what we agreed to do. Essentially it reflects values and standards. Consistency is about repetition — doing the same things over and over to reach a desired result or outcome.

Each of us can recall a time in our lives when we achieved a result that required consistent action. We set goals to get into school, set goals for the grades and degrees we wanted to earn, etc. We learned that all big things come from small beginnings of purposeful, consistent and meaningful actions.

As we begin to work on Milestone 3 — Consistency, I ask that you take the time to write down the answer to the following question: What one thing could you do right now, regularly, that would make a positive difference in the accomplishment of your Big Promise Goal — the goal that you wrote in Milestone 2?

We'll come back to this question after we put Milestone 3 in perspective.

Consistency is the steadfast adherence to the application of something. It is the reliability or uniformity of successive results. Being consistent helps you become successful by allowing you to see what works for you.[1]

WHY CONSISTENCY SHOULD BE A TOP PRIORITY

Consistency should be our top priority when reaching our goals because:

1. **It provides substance**. For example, my best friend and I agreed to try out a new face cream. I stopped using it for 3 days. She, on the other hand, used the cream for 30 days with outstanding results. I realized that I didn't have the same results because I had no realistic, consistent measurement. I didn't function at the same level as my friend. I intended to, but I didn't follow through. Intentions are not the same as results. No matter my excuse, I didn't consistently invest the time to have the same effects as my best friend. I had good intentions, but I didn't make those intentions real. No matter our purposes, if we don't start measuring our lives based on results, we'll continue to accept excuses from ourselves and others. We either need to walk the talk — not just in words, but also through actions — or stop making promises to ourselves and others that we don't keep. Period.

2. **It creates discipline.** Without discipline, you're relying on chance to achieve your goals, which is highly unlikely to happen in the timeframe you desire. Of course, I would have enjoyed the same results my friend received, but my

lack of discipline and my inconsistent application of the new face cream proved that I didn't create the discipline necessary for the same results. The truth of the matter is that we won't have the outcomes we want based on our intentions. We must create a consistent discipline to achieve real change, real results.

3. **It creates success.** By being substantive and disciplined, you can weed out what's not working. Consistency in action is the hidden key to success. It develops routines and builds momentum. It leads to habits that become second nature. And these habits inform the steps we take every day; they create the actions that lead to success. Consistent action is where the rubber meets the road. It's the moment of truth.

We all know that Olympic athletes such as Serena Williams train intensely every day. Similarly, we watch entertainers like Beyoncé, who perform flawlessly with their team of dancers and realize that it requires training. What makes these individuals different? Where does their relentless grit and motivation come from? What drives their consistency? Consider that it's something more than the accomplishment of a goal. If there is one thing I've learned in life, I believe it's about the power of using our voice.

Yes, Olympic athletes train to win the gold medal, but they also share their truth with the world. Who they become, and how they impact the world becomes just as important as their skill. The same is true for entertainers. It's not just about achieving world fame. As Michele Obama says, it's about "Becoming."

WHY IS CONSISTENCY SO HARD?

It's hard to be consistent because the struggle is real. In other words, the process to get to a result or outcome does not always produce a positive feeling. In fact, the journey can be challenging at times. Most of us quit during the struggle before we can experience the reward of staying the course. Staying the course requires consistent action.

Early in my career, I learned that consistency had to be part of my formula for success. Consistency was the only way to cope with the multiple demands of being a wife, mother and businesswoman. It doesn't matter if your goal is to become a member of your company's senior leadership team or to pitch your first presentation to an investment capitalist. Consistency is the determinant of success. It's how you'll accomplish your targeted goal — your Big Promise Goal.

In life, you must show up consistently. Because, as we all know, life happens. Some days will be more challenging than others. Not only does it take work to be consistent, you must also learn from your actions and grow from them.

In his book, *Peaks and Valleys*, Spencer Johnson's says:

> Not every day has to be amazing. It is natural for everyone everywhere to have peaks and valleys at work and in life.[2]

Through a short parable, Johnson explains the value of acknowledging that everyone has ups and downs. There's no shame in admitting that not every day is the best day ever. He believes that because everyone has ups and downs, it's the way we react to the changing landscape that makes the difference.

The whole idea of novelty is that some days need to be different to make them feel special. Johnson writes that the ups and downs help to provide a sense of balance and appreciation. If you didn't have cold, frozen winters, warm summer evenings wouldn't mean as much. So rather than trying to avoid your peaks and valleys, look at them with a broader perspective. Embrace your valleys, knowing that with time and work, you can be on your way to a better view.[3]

A FORMULA TO CONSISTENTLY TAKE ACTION

1. **Be present.**
   Being present is a gift you give to yourself. When you minimize distractions and consciously decide to engage in the task at hand, you seize the day and let go of the past to make room for the future.

2. **Embrace the peaks and valleys.**
   Acknowledge that everyone has ups and downs. Embrace your valleys, knowing that with time and work you'll be on your way to a better view. This acceptance serves as a natural barrier separating the quitters from those who go on to experience extraordinary success.

3. **Start again**. Even when life happens and you get off track towards your goal, remember you can always start again.

Now, back to my initial question:

What one thing could you do right now, on a regular basis that would make a positive difference in the accomplishment of your Big Promise Goal — the goal that you wrote in Milestone 2?

LET'S TAKE ACTION NOW

Develop a daily schedule for taking consistent action. This schedule will show that you are consistent in your actions. Then work to be present; embrace your peaks and valleys, and seize each day. For each of the next 60 days, name at least one seize-the-day moment that you can point to as relating to your Big Promise Goal.

TAKE CONSISTENT ACTION

SAMPLE (Monday - Sunday)

6:00 A.M.	Prayer/Meditation Time
7:00 A.M.	Yoga
8:30 A.M.	Office Work
10:00 A.M.	Meet with Banker (A seize the day moment)
12:00 P.M.	Lunch
1:00 P.M.	Office Work
2:00 P.M.	Write my "Culture Story" (A seize the day moment)
2:30 P.M.	Meet with a client (A seize the day moment)
3:00 P.M.	Team Meeting
5:00 P.M.	Home
7:30 P.M.	Read another chapter of Capacity Shatter the Limits — Now! (A seize the day moment)

Motivational
Milestone Map

Specific Measurable Results to Deliver Each Week

M | ap the ideas and concepts.
A | ct on initiatives.
P | rogress to results — to your next level dream.

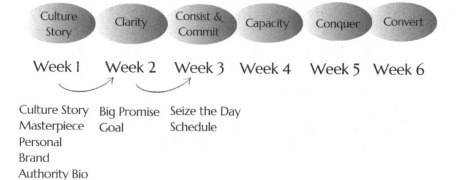

Culture Story	Big Promise	Seize the Day
Masterpiece	Goal	Schedule
Personal		
Brand		
Authority Bio		

MILESTONE THREE
Executive Summary

1. Consistency is the steadfast adherence to the application of something. It's the reliability or uniformity of continuous results.

2. Consistency is a determinant of success, the practical fulfillment of reaching your targeted goal — your Big Promise Goal.

3. There is no shame in acknowledging that not every day is the best day ever. Everyone has ups and downs. It's how we react to the changing landscape that makes the difference.

4. Embracing your peaks and valleys serves as a natural barrier separating the quitters from those who go on to experience extraordinary success.

5. To achieve your goal takes consistent action. When you take consistent action, life rewards those actions.

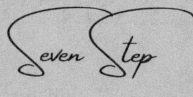

"C" FRAMEWORK

Culture
Story
Clarity
Consistency
Commitment
Capacity
Conquer
Convert

WHAT TRANSFORMS A PROMISE INTO REALITY

MILESTONE FOUR

Commitment
Come Through Time After Time

Motivation is what gets you started.
Commitment is what keeps you going.
Jim Rohn

"I don't like feeling trapped." That's how Jennifer said her job made her feel — trapped. When I asked her why she felt trapped, she said the long hours, the routine of the high volume of work required at the end of each month seemed never-ending. She felt like she had no control over her life and interacted very little with people. Her job in Accounting was all about the numbers. The day in/day out routine of the job made her feel invisible and powerless.

Before we began to work together, Jennifer said she could not begin to think about the future or imagine any action that would move her from where she was to where she wanted to be. She only knew that the current situation was no longer working and although she consistently went to work, she was no longer committed to the job. She described her experience as that of a hamster in a ball, repeating the same thing over and over.

Jennifer's experience shows us that you can be consistent and still not be committed. Don't get me wrong, Consistency is a fundamental determinant of success; it helps you stay the course. Yet, without commitment, consistency has no purpose. It's just a series of actions.

Abraham Lincoln said it best: Commitment is what transforms a promise into reality. Commitment is the words that speak boldly of your intentions and the actions which speak louder than words. It is making the time where there is none, coming through time after time, year after year. Commitment is the stuff character is made of — the power to change the face of things. It is the daily triumph of integrity over skepticism."[1]

You made a promise to yourself and others when you wrote your Big Promise Goal in Milestone 2. You'll need to approach this Big Promise Goal with consistency and commitment and as much grit as you can give. If you approach this goal with nothing more than an expanded awareness, you'll never get what you want.

LIFE HAPPENS AND WOMEN ARE BUSY

I'm keenly aware of the current state of things. Since the onset of the COVID-19 pandemic, many women have pushed aside the idea of having it all because they're busy doing it all. With all their doing, there's one thing women agree isn't happening: They're so busy, they aren't taking care of themselves.[2]

Decades of research shows that women do more housework and childcare than men — so much so that women who are employed full-time are often said to be working a "double-shift."[3] Now, women — mothers in particular — are taking on an even heavier load. Mothers are more than three times as likely as fathers to be responsible for most of the housework and caregiving during the pandemic. They are 1.5 times more likely than fathers to be spending an additional three or more hours per day on housework and childcare.[4]

Forty-two-year-old Linda is married with two children. She says that she burns out at the end of each day and is completely exhausted from being an executive, teacher, wife and childcare provider for her family. While her husband helps, his career requires that he be physically in the office four days a week. Her job is a bit more flexible, and she works full-time remotely since the pandemic struck. This flexibility in her job, she believes, has placed her in the position of bearing most of the family burden as it relates to the children.

> I feel like I'm barely surviving trying to keep all the balls in the air. I wish I had enough time and even the energy to take care of myself.

Experts say it's no surprise that women forget — or even disregard — the need to take care of themselves. The truth is, life happens. Yet, the airline industry has taught us what we need to do in an emergency. You need to put on your own oxygen mask before attending to others. When you take care of yourself first, you'll be better positioned to help others.

As women, we place everyone else first. When we learn to put ourselves first, we'll be better equipped to help ourselves and those around us. Recently, my Career Mastered Women's Leadership Network (a private online Facebook group of more than 1,200 women supporting women) hosted a panel discussion and asked women to share how women could Reset, Reclaim, Refocus and Reboot during the pandemic and beyond. Here are some of the key takeaways from the discussion:

1. Learn to dance in the rain by changing your mindset. There will be some rough days, but it takes just 15 minutes to go outside and breathe.

2. Set boundaries at home and work. There must be a timeout in the game.

3. Set roles and expectations with your employers and your family. If leading four projects is not possible, say so. If everyone isn't pitching in to help around the house, say so. Set up a plan where everyone has a role, including the children.

4. Put yourself at the top of the list and spend some time with yourself and for yourself. Self-care may be a nice bath with a glass of good wine or meditating, writing or praying.

5. Exercise, even if it's only for 15 minutes several times per week. It's healthy, and it'll relieve stress.

WHY COMMITMENT MATTERS TO YOUR GOALS

Commitment is not merely keeping the promise that you made to do something. It includes dedication, hard work and grit. Staying committed to your goal is one of the most fundamental principles of success. Most people commit for two or three months. A few people commit for two or three years. But a winner will commit for as long as it takes to win!

So, my question to you is: How long will you continue to make promises to yourself that you do not keep? As women, we tend to take care of everyone else before we take care of ourselves. Yes, I said, it, girl, enough is enough. When are you going to commit to you? You matter!

LET'S TAKE ACTION NOW

1. Decide on the process you are committed to practicing.

2. Refer to the book *Peaks & Valleys* by Spencer Johnson.

3. Select an accountability partner to help you stay motivated to your commitment.

Motivational Milestone Map

Specific Measurable Results to Deliver Each Week

M | ap the ideas and concepts.
A | ct on initiatives.
P | rogress to results — to your next level dream.

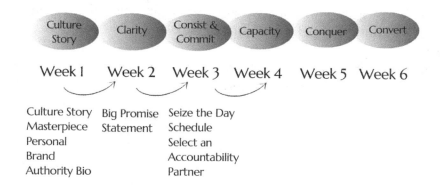

Week 1 — Culture Story, Masterpiece, Personal Brand, Authority Bio

Week 2 — Big Promise Statement

Week 3 — Seize the Day Schedule, Select an Accountability Partner

MILESTONE FOUR
Executive Summary

1. Commitment is what transforms a promise into reality.

2. The words that speak boldly of your intentions and the actions that speak louder than words give evidence of your commitment.

3. As women, we place everyone else first. When we learn to place ourselves first, we'll be better for ourselves and those we help.

4. Staying committed to your goal is one of the most fundamental principles of success.

5. Commitment is the stuff character is made of — the power to change the face of things.

Part Three

ADVANCE STRATEGIES

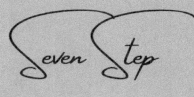

Seven Step

"C" FRAMEWORK

Culture
Story
Clarity
Consistency
Commitment
Capacity
Conquer
Convert

Capacity:

THE POWER TO PRODUCE, PERFORM, OR DEPLOY.
THE POWER TO DO IT NOW!

MILESTONE FIVE

Capacity
The Power to Do It Now!

What lies behind us and what lies before us are tiny
matters compared with what lies within us.
Ralph Waldo Emerson

I n 2011, my spouse and I decided to become quasi-snowbirds, travelling between Michigan and North Carolina because I had decided to leave the automotive industry and join big box retail. When I received the offer to join the senior leadership team of a new company, I knew my previous experience had prepared me for this moment. While deciding to take this opportunity, I had an epiphany — I suddenly understood the real meaning of the word "Capacity." Capacity is commensurate with opportunity. In short, you have the power to do it now!

I knew I was ready for the assignment; the timing was right. But like many of you, I questioned myself. I found myself almost drowning in the what-ifs. My new duties in a $53B company would include enterprise-wide responsibilities for 200,000 plus employees at 1,800 locations across the United States.

My mother — who was certainly beaming with pride — once said to me: Your journey has prepared you for this! You've done the pre-work. Essentially my Mom was saying that when

David killed the lion, he was expanding his Capacity so he could eventually kill the giant.

David's encounter with the lion occurred before his fight with Goliath. It's just possible that if he hadn't killed the lion, he might not have gotten the opportunity to fight Goliath. Most likely, he wouldn't have even qualified for the fight. His Capacity to fight the lion was an important steppingstone for David. The moral of the story? If you don't do anything with your lion, don't even think about the giant.

David knew he was ready.

He had quite a conversation with King Saul because he wanted to fight Goliath. King Saul wasn't sure if the teenager was up to the task of fighting this giant who was an experienced warrior. But David knew from experience that he could do it. He had worked in the field to keep the sheep safe, and he did so by killing the lion.

If you shatter the small things in front of you, you'll enlarge your Capacity to go after the bigger things just ahead.

CAPACITY IS THE POWER TO DO IT NOW

Capacity isn't potential. Potential means you just haven't done it yet. Capacity is the power to do it now. Can you imagine if David had said to King Saul, "I have the potential to slay the giant?" No, he told the King he had the power to do it now. He was sure of his Capacity to get the job done.

I've learned during my career that you have to work the level you're on so you can develop and maximize what you have to give. The 100-fold opportunity isn't coming until you do something with what you already have.

Today, in my consulting practice, most questions I receive from women are about getting ahead in their careers. Their questions focus on facing limiting beliefs and fears, such as, "I am not sure if I'm ready for this role." They may have to negotiate delicate situations with bosses and colleagues or weigh complicated career and life choices. Despite their fears and the obstacles facing them, these women want to move forward in life and in work.

And I agree. It's your time and your turn! Consider these truths: First, you've got what it takes. Second, you're worth the effort it will take to find the truth and create your goals and, third: Nobody is going to do it for you! Get busy!

So, let's review for a moment here:

1. You've written your Culture Story, which answers the questions: Who Am I? What's my identity? Why do people come to me for help? Who am I helping?

2. Next, you took action to write your personal brand authority biography — your Culture Story with your experience and expertise added.

3. You've also taken the time to determine your goals. You've prioritized your Big Promise Goal and wrote it down as a statement for later reference.

Now, what if you followed the CAPA© Method?

- To position your Culture Story
- To create a framework for your Big Promise Goal
- To make your goal actionable

ENSURING YOUR SUCCESS HABITS

My goal is to teach you how to use the 7-Step C Framework, which includes the CAPA Method. The value of this is that CAPA lifts your Capacity to transform your goals into reality, shattering limits that you've identified.

HOW TO USE THE CAPA METHOD

CAPA is defined as:

C̲ HOICES: It's about your decisions.

A̲ TTITUDE: It's about the mindset of being ready to get it done.

P̲ OSITIONING: It's about being in the circle and the power of proximity.

A̲ LTITUDE: It's about leveling to Capacity each day.

The CAPA Method focuses on how well you've mastered your Capacity to use your power now — without limits. So, let's look at each of the elements of the CAPA Method.

Choices: The key is to acknowledge and accept accountability for your life and decisions. You can make your goal actionable with the right decisions because you create your experiences. The behavior you choose is what becomes the results you have to work with.

Attitude: Mindset is key to how we behave and what we do. You must be real with yourself and ask the hard questions. Do I have a goal? Or, am I just going through the motions, day after day? Am I continuing to make promises to myself that I never keep? Or am I using my power to produce my goal.

Positioning: How and where we position ourselves matter. Be specific about your circles and everybody in it. Proximity is power.[1] You can join inner circles to rise to the next level.

Altitude: Your Attitude + your Aptitude = your Altitude. Check your attitude — mindset and behaviors — daily. Get accustomed to seizing the day. Do your homework, and stay abreast of your discipline, while keeping your eye on your Big Promise Goal — your North Star. You'll begin to deploy your Capacity, shatter limits and move from purpose to impact. Once you understand and use your daily Capacity, you'll realize that you're performing at the next level. The power of Capacity is that it can move up or down, depending on your mastery of CAPA. Remember that the key is to maximize your Capacity at each level. The 100-fold opportunity will not appear until you do something with what you already have.

Framework

CAPA© METHOD
FOR GOAL ACHIEVEMENT

Capacity

Focus on Mastery to Transform Dreams Into
Goals Into Outcomes, Shattering the Limits

TURN DREAMS INTO GOALS AND GOALS INTO OUTCOMES

Today, as I reflect on my time in corporate America and the journey I took to master my career, I realize that Capacity was at the center of it all. I fell many times and each time had to get back up. I often felt challenged being a wife, a mother of two and working a demanding job in a major corporation. But I decided early in my career that I had choices, and my choice was to remove the limits that I faced — especially the ones I was placing on myself. If anyone was going to stand up for me, it had to be me using every ounce of Capacity I could muster.

This Mississippi girl learned a lot from her Culture Story of "separate but equal." No matter how bleak life seems or what limits are placed upon you, there's always a way out, around or above the matter.

When I was a little girl, my grandfather and the community around me taught me about Capacity — the power to do it now. As an insurance salesman in the '60s back in Greenville, Mississippi, my grandfather never owned a car; instead, he walked the neighborhoods for miles each day, making his sales. He was a business professional who modeled leadership for his children and grandchildren.

Each morning, he would dress in his suit, tie and hat, and set out with his briefcase on his route, sometimes walking to the next city to sell insurance. One of my greatest treats was to walk him part of the way. At least, I thought that was what I was doing. Essentially, I walked one block with him, which was all my grandmother would allow so that she could keep me in her view. While walking, he would challenge my Capacity by merely asking me to keep up with his steps. He was a tall, statuesque man, and his strides were large. If I could keep up with him to the end of the block, he would give me a quarter — big money back then! At the age of seven, I would take three to four steps to keep up with his one stride. No matter. I kept up with him to the end of the block. My grandfather was teaching me how to use every ounce of my Capacity at that very moment. He was teaching me how to have a goal and use my power to achieve it.

Each time I walked with him, I got better and better at keeping up with his strides, and I received the Big Promise Goal — a quarter. That promise goal became my North Star. As I got older, Grandaddy, as we called him, told me, "It's how we look at things and react to them that matters." There we were living in the deep south, drinking out of water fountains that said "colored," yet not once in our home environment and community did my siblings and I feel we didn't have a choice. In fact, we felt just the opposite.

I learned early on that my purse is not my worth, and that human capital is golden. I was taught that giving up is not an option, that detours are needed for repairs and maintenance and that I have choices.

During my walks with my grandfather, he would share little nuggets about life. I've passed on to my children and grandchildren the one that carried me through many moments of my life and career journey. When the road gets tough — and it will — you need an anchor. My grandfather said always remember, Attitude + Aptitude = Altitude. I often repeated this mantra, and it helped me to succeed in both my career and my life. By keeping the right attitude and applying myself, I could up my level.

As I think about my years in corporate America, about being a wife for 40 years, a mother of two wonderful sons and now a grandmother of three, I reflect on how I used my Capacity. I used my power to do it now and made choices to transform my dreams into goals, and my goals into outcomes.

When women ask me how I mastered my career as a working mother and wife and find purpose, I tell them that when I chose to take my future into my own hands, I created what I wanted. You can too!

Are you ready to get clear on what you have to offer? We're about to connect your Culture Story and your personal brand authority to your Big Promise Goal — your North Star.

Remember: Capacity is the power to do it now!

 *What* if you followed a framework

Culture Story

Personal Brand Authority

North Star
Purpose to Impact

Big Promise Goal

Capacity

Now that you understand that the CAPA Method is a lever to get you from point A to point Z, you can prepare concise visual content that will take you from one step to the next. Using your Capacity to apply the steps outlined in this book will pull you forward and upward to your desired results. The key is to focus on the mastery of the actions, which are broken down into themes to lead to the desired outcome.

To help you visualize these next steps, here's the iconic pyramid representing Abraham Maslow's Hierarchy of Needs. It's probably a visual that you recognize:

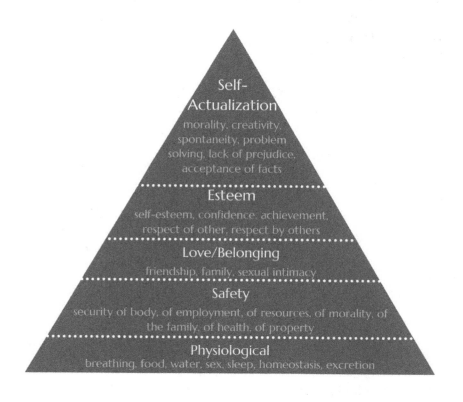

Source: Wikipedia.org

Abraham Maslow's theory is that humans have a series of needs, some of which must be met before they can turn their attention toward others. Certain universal needs are the most pressing, while more acquired emotions are of secondary importance.[1]

The order in which the needs are listed is not a coincidence. According to Maslow, physiological needs must be met first, before safety. Only after physiological and safety requirements are met will someone begin looking at those under belonging and love.[2]

The Capacity Altitude Pyramid© is based on a similar framework of a step-by-step ascension up the pyramid. Every level builds on itself, leading you toward your North Star — your Big Promise Goal.

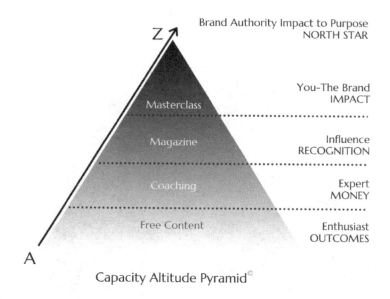

Capacity Altitude Pyramid©

Using my Masterclass as my North Star — Big Promise Goal, I developed my Capacity Altitude Pyramid©, starting with content or offerings that I, as the brand authority, provide to others. The first step up the ladder was to offer free content, such as blogs on women's leadership principles. At this stage, I was an enthusiast who might receive a thank-you or appreciation note as an outcome.

Building from this value step, I began to provide a coaching service as an expert, which I monetized. The next value offering was the publication of a woman's career magazine. It's here that I became an influencer and began to receive brand recognition. Now, I was ready to turn my attention to the Masterclass, which was my Big Promise Goal, to help high-achieving women break free so they could master their careers and create a life without limits. This was my North Star — the place where my brand authority shows up, where I use my Capacity to have value-added impact.

LET'S TAKE ACTION NOW

Now it's time to develop your Capacity Altitude Pyramid©.

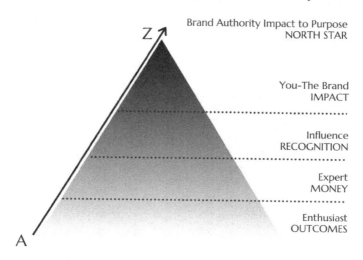

Motivational
Milestone Map

Specific Measurable Results to Deliver Each Week

M | ap the ideas and concepts.
A | ct on initiatives.
P | rogress to results — to your next level dream.

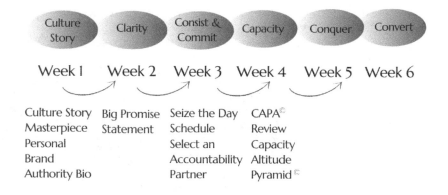

Week 1	Week 2	Week 3	Week 4
Culture Story	Big Promise	Seize the Day	CAPA©
Masterpiece	Statement	Schedule	Review
Personal		Select an	Capacity
Brand		Accountability	Altitude
Authority Bio		Partner	Pyramid©

MILESTONE FIVE
Executive Summary

1. Capacity is the power to do it now. It's not potential.

2. Capacity can move up or down, depending on your mastery of CAPA.

3. The CAPA Method focuses on your Capacity to use your power — now — without limits.

4. CAPA is defined as:
   C| HOICES: It's about your decisions.
   A| TTITUDE: It's about being ready to get it done.
   P| OSITIOING: It's about the power of proximity.
   A| LTITUDE: It's about measuring up to Capacity each day.

5. The 100-fold opportunity isn't coming until you do something with what you already have.

6. Using your Capacity to apply the steps outlined in this book will pull you forward and upward to your desired results. The key is to focus on mastery of the actions, which are broken down into themes that to the desired outcome.

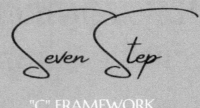

"C" FRAMEWORK

Culture
Story

Clarity

Consistency

Commitment

Capacity

Conquer

Convert

Conquer : GAIN A VICTORY OVER
SURMOUNT
MASTER
OVERCOME

MILESTONE SIX

Conquer
Start with the End in Mind

You have to believe in yourself when no one else does.
Serena Williams

Serena Williams is one of the best examples of a woman rising from humble beginnings to achieve the life of her dreams. I admire her perseverance, commitment and consistency to shatter all limits while using her Capacity to the fullest to conquer her goals. She says it doesn't matter how old or how young you are; you can achieve anything you put your mind to. As she said:

> I didn't grow up with things being handed to me.
> I had to work hard, I had to dedicate myself and
> I had to be determined.

Williams says that even outside sports, there's a requirement to be disciplined and most important, to believe.[1] Williams once said, "Because . . . some people might not believe in you, you have to believe in yourself." Williams explains that she has had people overlook her because she was a woman. Critics forecast that she would never win another Grand Slam.[2] Yet today, she is the world's number one tennis star because she worked hard, was determined, believed in herself and enlarged her Capacity to shatter limits and conquer her goals.

Serena Williams, the four-time Olympian, has played through many things: shoulder inflammation, knee injuries even pregnancy. She won the 2017 Australian Open while carrying her daughter Olympia. But what tennis fans didn't realize as she played her way towards 23 Grand Slam wins was that she was often dealing with an invisible pain: migraine headaches.[3] According to Williams, it was hard for her to explain to her dad, why the sunlight during her daily practices was causing her so much pain.[4]

Williams says there have been so many matches where she just had to power through her migraine attacks, like a 2001 match she lost to Martina Hingis in Sydney.

As I think about what it took to get to the finish line of securing my doctorate, I can identify with Williams. Anyone who knows me or works with me will tell you that I'm a noticeably confident woman. I am a successful founder and CEO of three organizations. Over my career, Fortune 50 companies have invited me to become a senior leadership team member. I have been responsible for the engagement of more than 200,000 employees of two of the world's largest companies. I have traveled in helicopters and company jets with the chairmen, CEOs and presidents of major corporations. I have given hundreds of speeches, including speaking to more than 800 women from across 90 countries in one setting in Korea. I've served as a member of the White House Commission for Historically Black Colleges and Universities and have been privileged to meet with several presidents of the United States.

Yet, I was challenged with doubt about securing my doctoral degree.

MANAGING COMPETING PRIORITIES

While enrolled in a doctoral program, I was promoted several times. Although this was great for my career, the timing was not ideal because with greater authority comes greater responsibility. Over time, my priorities had changed, and the course work became increasingly more challenging. I decided that I couldn't manage my job and focus on completing my doctorate. I contacted the Chair of my program to say that I could not continue in the program. I was struggling with competing priorities, and I thought it would be best to let go of the one that seemed to me beyond my reach. I didn't think I could manage my job, my family and my degree — all at the same time. But my Chair believed in me and encouraged me to get back on my game to power through to the end.

Are you ready to power through?

Are you tired of living paycheck to paycheck? Do you feel like you're stuck in a job wishing that you were proud of your career? Are you afraid of taking the leap to start your own business? Do you want more out of your next phase of life than what you're experiencing now?

Most of us want to live life to the fullest. Yet, we often settle for less. Why?

Why do we accept limits that could be shattered? Many of us are thirsty for meaning and purpose in our lives rather than taking life as it comes. We are high-achieving women who want to take charge of our lives and careers and see our goals accomplished according to our plans. Yet, we allow ourselves to remain stuck in a job that's going no where — or perhaps, we're succeeding and have become too comfortable to try something new that might be too risky.

START WITH THE END IN MIND

In Milestone Six, I want to help you conquer the promise you defined and made to yourself in Milestone Two. You defined it, working through the CAPA Method and the Capacity Altitude Pyramid. This is your action plan to get to your Big Promise Goal or, as I call it, your North Star — that place that allows you be true to your purpose.

I am persuaded that the best way to describe how to conquer your goal can be captured in one phrase: Shatter the excuses and limits by starting with the end in mind.

That phrase represents how to best focus on the achievement of your goals. Like Olympians, many of us have limits that must be shattered to conquer our goals.

If you want to succeed in life, you must passionately pursue your truth and apply it appropriately in your life. Your Culture Story is your truth. Using that story in every aspect of your life is vital.

The great Chinese philosopher, Lao Tzu, who founded Taoism which advocates living a simple life, summed it up as follows:

> . . . knowing others is intelligence, knowing yourself is true wisdom, mastering others is strength, but mastering yourself is true power.

Before you conquer your goal, you must master yourself and overcome any limits imposed by yourself or others. How do we accomplish this? By shattering them.

APPLY THE TTATS TO YOUR LIMITS

Sometimes we accept barriers that restrict us. But we don't have to. It's time to get real about your limits.

You'll need a notebook to do this work because you'll have action items to respond to in each section. The key is to be truthful about the reality of your limits. To get serious, you will need to employ TTATS. Make your limits:

Transparent
Track them
Analyze them
Test them
Shatter them

1. **Make the limits transparent**

Your first step is to understand what is meant by limits to a career or to life's success. On the journey of success, we often encounter limits that appear in many forms. While some of these limits will be obvious; others will not.

To identify your limits, let's start with your biggest pain points. What are they? Here are some examples of standard limits to success:

- Lack of time, money or resources that delay your actions
- Not believing in your own capability
- Inefficiencies such as lack of knowledge or skills

- Not knowing the right people or processes
- Distractions from completing your work

TAKE ACTION NOW

1. **Write your limits down so you can visualize them:**

Identifying your limits visually helps you achieve transparency.

Create a simple TATTS visual board with the columns:
Limitation Description.
Red Limits: like a brick wall or anchor.
Yellow Limits: slowly chipping away at the roadblock.
Green Limits: shattered

2. **Track and measure the effects of your limits.**

Once you've identified your limits, track and measure them consistently using your visual board. The key is to be conscious of your limits.

TAKE ACTION NOW

- Review the limits you've identified on your visual board
- How many times do they appear?
- What does it cost you, in time or money?
- What isn't valued added when this limit appears?

Accept that you won't be able to immediately identify all your limits. But, in time, you'll see them all. Meanwhile, tackle the ones that present themselves first as being important. Then move to the next.

3. **Develop a plan of action**

Steps 1 and 2 identified your limits. Knowing what they are, you can develop a plan of action for shattering them. Remember that perspective is how you approach a problem. Seeing things from various sides is good. So, let's go.

TAKE ACTION NOW

- **What will happen if you don't change what you've been doing?** Think about continuing to live with your current situation. Even if you're willing to change, you've got to come up with a way to shatter your limit.

- **Could you solve this problem through negotiations?** We often impose limits on ourselves, instead of thinking whether someone else is involved. Consider your limit and analyze it. Is it self-imposed or imposed by others? Where can you negotiate?

- **Test your theory.** Ask for input from colleagues, partners, etc., so you can develop a way to remove your limits. Ask these questions:

TAKE ACTION NOW

- What are you thinking of doing about removing the limit?

- Paint a picture of success when the limit is removed. What does it look like?

- What solutions have you already tried?

4. Shatter, remove and move forward.

Be willing to take direct action to shatter your identified limits, based upon the solutions you tested. This may involve getting out of your comfort zone and pushing hard against the status quo. This may also include taking risks — asking for forgiveness rather than permission. This may require building a case for change and a coalition of support, which could take a lot of time and effort.

Take the time to do this right. You don't have to accomplish the entire process overnight. My suggestion is to give yourself several days to complete the work. The key is to make a commitment to yourself about when you expect to have this work completed.

Keep reviewing your TTATS Visual Board so you can prioritize how to shatter your limits.

I learned that my success depended on my visualizing the future before it came to pass. People who consistently win know what they want and get what they want. They visualize it, feel it and experience it by starting with the end in mind. Here's how to accomplish that.

Visioning the future

You know what you want — you've already developed your Big Promise Goal. So, look at your written goal and your Capacity Altitude Pyramid action steps.

Start with the end in mind

Visualize to affirm your success. Close your eyes and imagine yourself one year from now, having accomplished the Big Promise Goal. Whom did you help? Remember, this is not just about you. It's about serving others too. What does it feel like now that you've accomplished your goal? What are you doing?

Who are you with? How are you reacting? Are you celebrating? How do you know you've achieved your goal?

How does success change how you view yourself? Now walk your way back from the success picture to the start.

You must provide detailed answers to these questions and affirm your success as if it is already accomplished.

Desired Goal

Vision   Future

Success is not just about where you want go and what you want to achieve. It's also about how you get there. Successful people have a clear strategy for getting to the future they envision. I call these people winners because they plan the way to their goals. They have a map and timeline like the 7-Step C Framework. They're sure of what they want and go about the business of getting it done. They have a written strategy to their promise goal, which allows them to stay on track. They work on the elephants rather than the ants and stay on course by keeping their eyes on the North Star.

Now, let's convert the goal into outcomes.

LET'S TAKE ACTION NOW

Review Milestone 6 to ensure you've taken these actions:

1. Made the limit transparent.
2. Tracked the effects of limits.
3. Planned how to remove the limits.
4. Tested your solutions.
5. Shattered your limits and moved forward.

TATTS Visual Management Board
Limitation Analysis

Name Limit	Describe Limit	How Often Does It Occur?	Red Limit: Brick Wall	Yellow Limit: Slow Road Block	Green Limit: Shatter	Comments e.g. cost, time, money

Motivational
Milestone Map

Specific Measurable Results to Deliver Each Week

M | ap the ideas and concepts.
A | ct on initiatives.
P | rogress to results — to your next level dream.

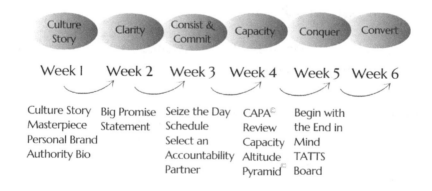

Week 1	Week 2	Week 3	Week 4	Week 5	Week 6
Culture Story	Big Promise	Seize the Day	CAPA©	Begin with	
Masterpiece	Statement	Schedule	Review	the End in	
Personal Brand		Select an	Capacity	Mind	
Authority Bio		Accountability	Altitude	TATTS	
		Partner	Pyramid©	Board	

MILESTONE SIX
Executive Summary

1. We're high-achieving women who want to take charge of our lives and careers and see our goals accomplished according to our plans.

2. Sometimes we accept limits that restrict us.

3. Having identified these limits and visualized them, I can now prioritize how to shatter them.

4. To conquer my goal, I'll imagine myself one year from now, having accomplished it.

5. Now I'll walk backward from the success picture to start the action plan to my goal.

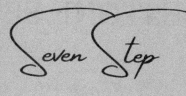

Seven Step

"C" FRAMEWORK

Culture
Story

Clarity

Consistency

Commitment

Capacity

Conquer

Convert

Convert:

CAUSE TO CHANGE, INFORM, OR FUNCTION

MILESTONE SEVEN

Convert
Driving for Results That Matter

She believe she could so she did.
R.S. Grey

I n this final chapter of your preparation for mastering your career and life, you'll learn how to turn your Big Promise Goal into results. Successful women convert their goals into results, by building on what they've accomplished.

One of the most significant limitations to success is maintaining the game level that got you there in the first place. Just read the book, *What Got You Here Won't Get You There* by Marshall Goldsmith,[1] How does Serena Williams maintain the level of athleticism that won her the first Grand Slam? How can a best-selling artist guarantee that her next artwork will be as successful as the last? How can a college student who just earned that bachelor's degree guarantee that she can monetize its purpose? How does a successful corporate executive consistently leverage results?

WOMEN LEADING THE WORLD TO 2030

In 2015, governments worldwide stepped up and agreed to achieve 17 Sustainable Development Goals, otherwise known as the Global Goals, by 2030.[2] These Global Goals and their 169 component targets have been designed to create the kind of future most people want, one in which there's no poverty, the planet is protected and all people enjoy peace and prosperity.[3] The goals include achieving gender equality, empowering all women and girls and eliminating all forms of discrimination and violence against them. For companies that understand — and seize upon — the opportunities, the Global Goals represent more than $12 trillion (US) across key economic areas and up to 380 million jobs by 2030.[4]

These are big and audacious goals during challenging times. According to the report, the uncertainty resulting from today's environmental and social strains makes it hard for business leaders to see the way ahead. In addition, they're likely to face strong headwinds from those who are reaping benefits from an economy that at times seems to be reinforcing inequality and environmental destruction.[5]

"Behind Every Global Goal: Women Leading the World to 2030" celebrates the role women are playing to meet the 2030 deadline and makes a case for more women leaders to step forward and advocate for the future we want. The paper provides facts on the impact of gender-balanced teams and women leaders as they affect achieving the Global Goals.[6]

I've selected a few of the women in the Career Mastered Women's Leadership Network who serve as role models. They drive sustainability through their businesses in different sectors. This is just a small sampling of inspirational stories about creating an inclusive economy by converting goals into sustainable results.

WOMEN LEADERS TO INSPIRE US ALL

Profile One: Gail Perry-Mason
Senior Director of Investments at Oppenheimer & Co., Inc and Founder, Money Matters for Youth

Gail Perry-Mason, lifelong Detroiter, has come a long way from foster care. Not only is she a respected authority in the financial industry working as a senior director of investments at Oppenheimer & Co. Inc., one of the nation's largest investment firms, she's also a bestselling author.

Gail was adopted at the age of three. She was considered hard to place because of special needs. According to the adoption agency, she would never walk or talk. Today, a mother of three grown sons, she walks and talks exceptionally well. She is an inspirational leader who says it began with the love and nurturing she received from her adoptive parents.

She's passionate about mentoring and educating the next generation on financial literacy. Each year, she hosts Money Matters for Youth, a one-week camp that teaches children financial literacy, instructing over 6,000 young people in the Detroit-Metro area and mentoring more than 25 young women who are now professionals in the financial industry.

Money Matters has taught the core values of financial awareness and literacy, developing diverse, positive relationships and entrepreneurship, while emphasizing a message of giving back through service and philanthropy. Its goal is to provide a program committed to fostering young people's social, emotional and cognitive growth while preparing them for professional and personal success.

Gail's program has received national recognition, with Money Matters receiving an invitation from Warren Buffett to be the first youth group to attend the Berkshire-Hathaway Shareholder Meeting. It was also featured in a national documentary on Mr. Buffett, in 2017.

Gail Perry-Mason conducts workshops for employees of companies like Chrysler, IBM, MGM, McDonald's, DTE Energy, Blue Cross Blue Shield of Michigan and Wells Fargo — to name just a few. She took her wealth of wisdom to the airwaves when she co-hosted Building Wealth and an award-winning radio talk show broadcasted on Comcast Cable. She's appeared on national outlets such as BET, Fox News, PBS, CNN, MSNBC and NPR Radio.

To make her financial insights available to families like her, Gail wrote and published her first book, *Money Matters for Families,* which Chrysler employees used to get their household finances in order and helped them build strong financial foundations. Her second book, *Girl, Make Your Money Grow* was a national bestseller. In addition to her books, Gail has published locally and nationally in *Ebony, Black Enterprise, On Wall Street, Quick and Simple — Good Housekeeping* Magazine, *Essence, Jet, The Detroit Free Press, Detroit News, Signature, HER* Magazine, *Washington Post* and *Oprah's Debt Diet.*

In addition to her program, Money Matters for Youth, Gail serves her community on the Board of Directors for nonprofits such as The Salvation Army, Hutzel Harper Hospital, Neighborhood Services Organization and many more.

She's received many accolades from groups like Ford Motor Company, Michigan Women's Foundation, Alpha Kappa Alpha Sorority, Inc., Bank of America, Alternatives for Girls, Michigan's

Top 10 Businesswomen and Career Mastered Women's History Leadership in Action.

For more about Money Matters for Youth, visit her website **www.moneymattersforyouth.com**.

Profile 2: Sidney Bonvallet
Co-Founder and President of Helping Hands Touching Hearts (HHTH), and CJ Christopher, Co-Founder and Vice President

Helping Hands Touching Hearts is a nonprofit charity launched in 2008 by Sidney Bonvallet and CJ Christopher, a mother-daughter dynamic duo. Sidney's journey to founding HHTH did not follow a linear path. A former auto executive, business owner and public speaker, she and CJ started HHTH to serve South Africa and Zimbabwe. Their passion was to change poverty to prosperity and awaken hope.

The mission of HHTH is to empower impoverished people through sustainability with education, food, health and hope.

Both CJ and Sidney work with the Venda in Mutale, South Africa, and with the Shona and Ndebele in Zimbabwe. These are impoverished areas with 90% unemployment. The Venda people are willing to work to change their conditions. Schools function with the barest of essentials. The people need help with the basics, such as more classrooms, school supplies and equipment. They need medical assistance, help to manage farm projects and skills training.

HHTH's four initiatives are:

Education

In S. Africa, HHTH partnered with Fethani High School Principal, Gilbert Mbedzi, to build a STEM & VOC LAB for the children. Educational and entrepreneurial projects are a way to rise above a destiny of poverty.

Food

HHTH has a food program for the orphans in S. Africa and Zimbabwe. Sponsors donate the resources needed to feed about 130 orphan children every year. Most of the orphans HHTH works with survive on one meal a day. It makes concentration hard, yet they know they must get their education. HHTH also feeds impoverished elderly.

Health

Since malaria takes one life every minute in this area, HHTH wanted to start a mission to protect the villages' pregnant women and children because they are the most susceptible to this danger. HHTH supplies about 250 mosquito nets per year for pregnant women and children in these high-risk malaria areas and gives orphans soap, shampoo and basic hygiene supplies. Additionally, HHTH started the menstrual pads ministry for young ladies. Each one receives three washable, reusable pads; over 600 pads per year are distributed.

Hope

HHTH distributes clothing, shoes and undergarments to children and adults yearly. The charity has also built a children's care center in Masisi, S. Africa. This care center serves as a haven, a distribution center for food and clothing and a children's playground.

HHTH realizes that it cannot meet all the needs of its six adopted villages, 70 orphans in South Africa and 60 orphans and elderly in Zimbabwe. However, it is possible to help them get an education and bring joy to their hearts with food, clothes, shoes and some play.

The Zimbabweans are highly intelligent and strive to better their conditions through hard work and creativity. They rely on their abilities without a sense of entitlement. The Venda are peaceful and contented people; they believe in God's providence. HHTH intends to help both groups create a more bearable life, without detracting from the cohesiveness, purity and charm of their culture.

The investments made by contributors since 2008 have not only put smiles on the faces of villagers and hope in their hearts but have made a huge, sustainable social and economic impact. For more Information on HHTH, refer to: **www.clotheavillagenow.com.**

CONNECTING RESULTS TO PERFORMANCE

In each of these inspiring stories, we see how goals can be converted into powerful performance outcomes for impact and legacy. The key is to understand the link between the goal's objective and performance outcomes.

Most high-achieving women have a big, courageous goal. One aspires to become the next C-level executive promoted within the organization where she's employed; another dreams of making her brand more popular than the next; yet another longs to see the company she founded go global. They hope that their bold goals will become realities, with the imagined outcomes. To that end, they write vision statements, deliver speeches, and launch change initiatives. They devise procedures and create all the bells and whistles to ensure success. But often, these activities create layer upon layer of bureaucracy — limiting their ability to convert their results to sustainable outcomes.

Sometimes our quest for the North Star puts us in the busy-to-busy mode without translating our Big Promise Goal to an outcome. After three decades of working in corporate America, I have observed, studied and utilized a simple method to convert my goals into results like those in the case studies. Today, I recommend to my clients this potent yet straightforward managerial tool that helps women turn goals into outcomes and results that matter.

When talking to my clients, I learn that many have set a targeted goal or have been asked to hit a targeted goal without knowing how to use the bow and arrow. My simple question is that if you've conquered the goal, let's say, for example, your bachelor's degree, what are you going to do to convert the degree into an impactful outcome? In other words, in more simple terms, how do you ensure that the degree will add value?

In this book, I've already given you six of the seven steps to accomplish the promised goal you've made to yourself. In this final milestone, you're ready to convert your Big Promise Goal to outcomes.

YOUR OUTCOME TO IMPACT IN THIS WORLD.

PROMISE GOAL
MY GUIDING PURPOSE

<u>MILESTONES</u>
7 major steps to convert your Big Promise Goal to outcomes.

C onvert
A ctions
R esults
T o

Outcomes

7. Convert

6. Conquer

5. Capacity

4. Commitment

3. Consistency

2. Clarity

1. Culture Story

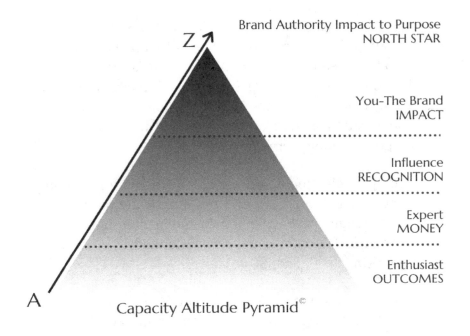

Capacity Altitude Pyramid©

Z — Brand Authority Impact to Purpose NORTH STAR

You-The Brand IMPACT

Influence RECOGNITION

Expert MONEY

Enthusiast OUTCOMES

A

GETTING TO OUTCOMES

The first step in your action plan is to distinguish between inputs, activities, outputs and outcomes to convert your goal into results. Outcomes measure the actual value you're creating, like financial growth — they are the keys to high performance. Paying attention to outcomes pays off in significant ways.

When we started the 7-step C Framework, we began with Milestone 1 — your Culture Story — which is critical for Capacity strengthening. Your Culture Story, as I defined it, is who you are and provides the bridge to your Personal Brand Authority message and from there to your Big Promise Goal. We further discussed that your Big Promise Goal would not only be about you but also the people you help — equally essential parts of your legacy.

To facilitate converting the Big Promise Goal into the ultimate impact outcome, I introduce my clients to a Logic Model. The logic model dates to Joseph S. Wholey who used the term in "Evaluation: Promise and Performance." This systematic and visual way to understand the activities planned and the results to be achieved measures success and identifies the value add of your goal for long term impact.[7]

Essentially, Logic Models are actionable plans with detailed steps for actively pursuing and systematically adding value for impact. Logic methods emphasize expected outcomes, so that unintended outcomes may be overlooked. In other words, we're working on elephants, not ants.

DIMENSIONS OF A LOGIC MODEL
Illustration- W.K. Kellogg Foundation, 2004

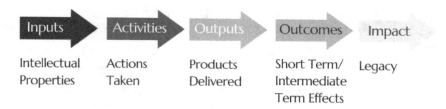

The dimensions of a logic model include: inputs, activities, outputs, outcomes and ultimate impact.[8]

A Logic Model flows from the left to the right, moving from the process side to the impact side. It identifies:

Inputs
Inputs are the resources available for the goal, such as funding, human resources, intellectual properties, including evidence-based strategies and partnerships. [9]

Activities

Activities include what's needed to bring about the intended result, such as forming a partnership to strengthen Capacity and develop research.[10]

Outputs

Outputs are the products or direct services resulting from the activities — evidence of implemented actions. It's important to differentiate between outputs and outcomes. Outputs relate to what's been done, whereas outcomes refer to what's different because of what's been done. Some examples are training, publishing a magazine, building a school establishing a nonprofit.[11]

Outcomes

Outcomes are the results expected. Short-term outcomes represent the most immediate effects that can be attributed to the achievement of the goal, such as changes in learning, knowledge and attitudes.[12] Examples include: knowledge and awareness of advancing women leadership within a community, and referral and mentoring at local school districts. Intermediate outcomes represent behaviors that are changed as a result of increased knowledge and awareness; for example, an increased number of girls making more informed decisions about becoming the first in their household to attend college.

Ultimate impact outcome

This refers to the long-term outcome; in other words, how the lives of beneficiaries of the goal changed due to inputs, activities, outputs, and outcomes .[13] Example: An educated society.

Assumptions

Assumptions are facts or conditions necessary for success. Your goal needs these conditions to succeed, but you believe these conditions already exist — they are not something you need to bring about with your activities. They are not within your control.[14]

External factors

External factors are the environment that may have a significant influence on your ability to convert your goal into outcomes and can come from individuals, organizations or groups.[15]

Logic

MODEL DEFINITIONS

Inputs

These are the resources for your program

e.g. Staff, Partnerships, Infrastructure, Support

Activities

What you do with the resources

e.g. Training

e.g. Development of Guidelines

Outputs

These are the direct products of the project's activities

e.g. Training Workshops, Handbook on Guidelines

ASSUMPTIONS

Short Term Outcomes

These are changes in learning

e.g. Knowledge, Attitudes, Awareness, Opinions, Motivations

Intermediate Outcomes

These are changes in action

e.g. Behavior, Procedures, Practice Policies, Decisions, Social Action

Impact

These are changes in conditions/situations as a result of the intervention

e.g. Social, Economic, Civic, Health, Environmental

EXTERNAL FACTORS

In 2015, I established a nonprofit to support and advance the next generation of girls' leadership and careers. A case study example of a Logic Model approach to produce a stated outcome is below.

LOGIC MODEL: A LEARNING NONPROFIT

Career Mastered Women's Leadership Network is the Catalyst for Excel Village Center for Learning. Excel Village will enhance the careers, literacy and other life skills among girls in grades 5 through 12 in various cities. The organization will provide scholarships, mentoring, and resources in science, technology, engineering, math, finance, arts and business.

For example, those who teach and provide girls with mentoring and career guidance are role models who demonstrate what a winning future looks like and the various career options available. The primary deliverable will be a structured mentoring program enabled by trained women in collaboration with specific school districts. The center will invest resources in mentoring clubs within various schools. This is more likely to increase a girl's interests and success. These resources will provide scholarships and pay for digital resources, including mentoring, science, technology engineering, math, finance, arts business (STEM-FAB) workbooks, videos, presentations and other low-cost content that will allow students to create a successful future.

LET'S TAKE ACTION NOW

We're now ready to actively pursue value-added outcomes by converting your Big Promise Goal into an actionable plan with detailed steps. I've provided Logic Model examples and a template for your use on the following pages.

MODEL DEFINITIONS EXAMPLES

Inputs	Activities	Outputs
Finance/Funding Infrastructure/ Venue	Group Work	Presentations
	Summit Curriculum Development	Exercises
Mentors		Facilitation
50 Girl Students	Team Observations	Summit Curriculum
Project Manager		

ASSUMPTION All 50 girl students will receive scholarships to attend the Summit.

Short Term Outcomes	Intermediate Outcomes	Impact
Changes in learning	Continued primary and secondary schooling in STEM-FAB related fields	More girls enrolled and completing STEM-FAB and related fields
Increased knowledge and awareness of STEM-FAB curriculum		

EXTERNAL FACTORS Students remain interested in STEM-FAB curiculum, summit, and clubs.

MODEL

CONVERT YOUR BIG PROMISE GOAL

Inputs	Activities	Outputs

ASSUMPTION

Short Term Outcomes	Intermediate Outcomes	Impact

EXTERNAL FACTORS

Motivational Milestone Map

Specific Measurable Results to Deliver Each Week

M | ap the ideas and concepts.
A | ct on initiatives.
P | rogress to results — to your next level dream.

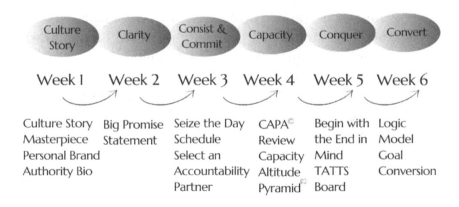

Week 1	Week 2	Week 3	Week 4	Week 5	Week 6
Culture Story	Big Promise	Seize the Day	CAPA©	Begin with	Logic
Masterpiece	Statement	Schedule	Review	the End in	Model
Personal Brand		Select an	Capacity	Mind	Goal
Authority Bio		Accountability	Altitude	TATTS	Conversion
		Partner	Pyramid©	Board	

MILESTONE SEVEN
Executive Summary

1. Turning goals into results is the power of conversion.

2. Conquering a goal is not the end game. The key is to understand the link between the goal's objective and performance outcomes.

3. Sometimes our quest for the North Star puts us in the busy-to-busy mode without translating our Big Promise Goals to an outcome.

4. Logic methods rest on well-reasoned approaches to how and why the model will produce the stated outcomes, so unintended outcomes may be eliminated.

5. With each of the 7 Steps building on each other, you are ready to convert your Big Promise Goal into outcomes.

EPILOGUE
"From Now On."

"From Now On."

A new beginning is when the past is seen as a prelude and nothing more. When we allow what has passed to no longer confine us, constrain us or hold us back, the past then becomes just that, the past.

As a prelude, it should become an impetus for further movement and seed for what needs to be done. Sometimes we can become a prisoner of the past. We get comfortable with what is and what used to be. Yesterday, last week, last year can prevent or stifle us from moving forward unless we decide to use these words "From Now On."

Let's start with the word "From" as it's the door that opens newness. It's a liberating word, representing a springboard, a launching pad, a starting point — a new beginning. "From" gives us the impetus to go forward and put things behind us. "From" provides us with motive power, a propelling instrument to go to where you need to go. Everything starts with "From Now On."

It's significant and paradoxical a new beginning starts with a departure. Using "From" as a first word is an opportunity to see it as a stepping stone. That's what happens when your step begins with "From." When you come through the door with "From" on your mind, you aren't captured there. You aren't held back because "From" is the initiating word. When you get out of bed and have "From" on your mind, you're going somewhere.

When "From" becomes your first word, you can start the day with action. It's a new beginning — a point of departure that is not defined by anything other than location. "From Now On."

The second word helps us appreciate that you don't have to start at a location to have the beginning of a significant venture. That's why the second word for consideration is "Now."

From *Now*. You don't have to leave town. It's "Now." Sometimes you must have a location to receive a new experience and start somewhere different. You can't get to someplace without going someplace else. You can't get to New York City from Jackson, Mississippi, by airplane without going somewhere else first. Jackson is not a hub city like Chicago. The only way I can get there is to change aircraft in another town. So, I can always say you can't get there from Jackson as a location.

But when the matter of departure is about time, you aren't cramped, constrained or confined. That's why Paul said in the Bible, "From Now On," meaning that his point of departure could start anywhere. He didn't have to wait to get to a certain location before beginning a fresh point.

"From Now On" — from this place. Paul didn't say he had to go to Jerusalem before starting a new beginning or beginning this new understanding. He said, "From Now On."

Just as he did, you can make up your mind right now. Today could be a whole new day:

- I will start to write that book, right now.
- I will start to work on my degree, right now.
- I will be positive with others, right now.
- I will join church, right now.
- I will start my new business, right now.

You don't have to wait until you get home or until tomorrow to start "From Now."

The newness in which you speak means it's "Now." You don't have to go anywhere else if you want to start fresh right now. It just takes time. Time is an important factor for forwarding movement. At a specific moment — a decision — a difference is to be made. Can this be the day? Can this be the moment? Right now.

Now is the acceptable time. It can happen anywhere if the time is acceptable, crucial and critical for what you deem needs to be done. It can happen anywhere when the time comes. When "Now" is on hand, it makes no difference where. It can happen anywhere — when the time comes. Now is the time.

At this moment in time — "Now" — new perspectives can take place. Given what I have going for me, good or bad, I'm going on anyway.

Now means any other considerations will not deter me. I've made up my mind — "From Now On." This moment — this time — not next time. Don't worry about last time (that's not Now). Don't worry until next year. Do it now. The decisive period is at hand. There's no telling what might happen. The prelude, the preliminarily, is wrapped up at this moment. Don't look back, don't delay. Some believe that the great moment was yesterday. Others believe it's going to happen later on. "From Now On," says we wait no more for a distant moment of movement to take place. It occurs Now. From your point of departure to Now — your moment of decisiveness is at this present moment. "Now" sets you up for the movement to the next word. If your decision is "From Now On," you need a launching pad to get over to "On."

"Now is the launching pad, your steppingstone. You can't get to "On" until you deal with "Now. If you haven't been to "Now," you can't go to "On" "Now" leads you to "On." If you missed the urgency of "Now" or keep delaying what you ought to be doing — get with "Now" Grab hold of "Now." Let 'Now" be your transition.

If "From" is the beginning and "Now" is about time, "On" is infinity. You're not just saying to stop here today. When dark clouds come, you're going "On." When deep valleys come, you're going "On." When the days are bright, you're going "On." That is the motivating force. When we know what "On" means, we can go forward, "From Now On!"

NOTES

MY VISION

1. Vanessa Fuhrmans, *Wall Street Journal*. Where Are All The Women CEOs? February 6, 2020. https://www.wsj.com/articles/why-so-few-ceos-are-women-you-can-have-a-seat-at-the-table-and-not-be-a-player-11581003276?mod=e2tw.

2. McKinsey & Co., *Women in the Workplace 2020*, September 30, 2020. https://www.mckinsey.com/featured-insights/diversity-and-inclusion/women-in-the-workplace.

3. McKinsey & Co., *Women in the Workplace 2020*, September 30, 2020. https://www.mckinsey.com/featured-insights/diversity-and-inclusion/women-in-the-workplace.

4. McKinsey & Company, *The Shortlist, Our Best Ideas, Quick & Curated*, October 16, 2020. https://www.mckinsey.com/~/media/McKinsey/Email/Shortlist/107/20 20-10-16.html#:~:text=This%20was%20most%20pronounced%20in,the%20 numbers%20were%20slowly%20improving.

5. US News, *Covid-19 Could Set women Back Decades on Gender Equality*. April 6, 2020 .https://www.usnews.com/news/best-countries/articles/2020-04-06/commentary-coronavirus-pandemic- may-set-women-back-decades-on-equality.

MILESTONE 1

1. Y Studios, *I Am . . . What Factors Influence Identity*, 7/2/2020. https://ystudios.com/insights-people/influence-on-identity.

2. Gallup, *Transform Great Potential into Greater Performance*. https://www.gallup.com/cliftonstrengths/en/252137/home.aspx.

3. Indeed.com, *List Hobbies & Interests on Your Resume* (with Examples), 3/14/2020. https://www.indeed.com/career-advice/resumes-cover- letters/listing-hobbies-and-interests-on-your-resume-with-examples.

4. Glantz.net, *How Does Your Personality Fascinate Others*. https://glantz.net/blog/how-does-your-personality-fascinate-others/.

5. Heidi Medina, *Why It Is Important to Celebrate Wins*, August 15, 2019. https://www.talktoheidi.com/why-its-important-celebrate-your-wins/.

6. Awilda Rivera, *6 Challenges in Life You Must Overcome to Become A Better Person*. https://www.lifehack.org/848700/challenges-in-life.

MILESTONE 2

1. Pareto Principle. https://en.wikipedia.org/wiki/Pareto_principle.

2. Indeed.com, Career Guide, SMART Goals, Definitions & Examples, October 20, 2020. https://www.indeed.com/career-advice/career-development/smart-goals.

MILESTONE 3

1. Dictionary.com. https://www.dictionary.com/browse/consistency.

2. Spencer Johnson, M.D., *Peaks & Valleys*, New York, NY, Atria Books.

3. Spencer Johnson, M.D., *Peaks & Valleys*, New York, NY, Atria Books.

MILESTONE 4

1. Sparkpeople.com, *A Great Quote About Commitment from Abraham Lincoln*, February 25, 2010. https://www.spark people.com/mypage_public_journal_individual.asp? blog_id=2925515#:~:text=%22COMMITMENT%20is%20 what%20tran sforms%20a,speak%20louder%20than%20 the%20words.

2. McKinsey & Co., *Women in the Workplace 2020*, September 30, 2020 https://www.mckinsey.com/featured-insights/ diversity-and- inclusion/women-in-the-workplace.

MILESTONE 5

1. Wikimedia Commons https://commons.wikimedia.org/ wiki/File:Maslow%27s_hierarchy_of_ne eds.svg.

2. Saul McLeod, Maslow's Hierarchy of Needs, March 20, 2020. https://www.simplypsychology.org/maslow.html.

MILESTONE 6

1. Serena Williams, Believe in You Video Transcript. August 26, 2016. https://www.goalcast.com/2016/08/26/serena-williams-importance-believing/.

2. Serena Williams, Believe in You Video Transcript. August 26, 2016. https://www.goalcast.com/2016/08/26/serena-williams-importance-believing/.

3. Julie Mazziotta and Eileen Finay, People.com, Serena Williams Has Struggled with Migraines for Years: I Got use to Playing Through the Pain. August 5, 2020. https://people.com/health/serena-williams- struggled-with-migraines-for-years/.

4. Julie Mazziotta and Eileen Finay, People.com, Serena Williams Has Struggled with Migraines for Years: I Got use to Playing Through the Pain. August 5, 2020. https://people.com/health/serena-williams- struggled-with-migraines-for-years/.

5. Serena Williams Opens Up About 'Debilitating' Migraines: "I Got Used To Playing Through The Pain' Chelsea Ritschel, Independent.co.uk., New York, August 5, 2020. https://www.independent.co.uk/life-style/serena-williams-migranes-pain-headache-tennis-a9655751.html.

MILESTONE 7

1. Marshall Goldsmith, *What Got You Here won't Get You There.* New York, NY. Hyperion.

2. The United Nations, *Take Action for the Sustainable Development Goals- United Nations Sustainable Development.* https://www.un.org/sustainabledevelopment/sustainable -development- goals/.

3. The United Nations, *The Global Goals for Sustainable Development.* https://www.globalgoals.org/.

4. Women Rising 2030, *Better Leadership, Better World: Women Leading for global Goals*, March 5, 2018, London. http://businesscommission.org/news/better-leadership-better-world.

5. The United Nations, *Transforming our world: the 2030 Agenda for Sustainable Development.* https://sdgs.un.org/2030agenda.

6. *Business & Development Sustainable Commission, Behind Every Global Goal: Women Leading the World to 2030, Discussion* September 2017. http://s3.amazonaws.com/aws-bsdc/BSDC_Behind-Every-Gobal-Goal.pdf.

7. Logic Model: The Roadmap to Change, Origins and Descriptions. HL250. Maureen, Rebecca, Hayley & John. http://logicmodel.weebly.com/origins-and-descriptions.html.

8. Logic Model Development Guide: Using Logic Models to Bring Together Planning Evaluation and Action, January 2004. https://www.aacu.org/sites/default/files/LogicModel.pdf.

9. Office of Astronomy for Development, Logic Model, Sahar Mohy-Ud-Din, OAD fellow. http://www.astro4dev.org/logic-model/.

10. Office of Astronomy for Development, Logic Model, Sahar Mohy-Ud-Din, OAD fellow. http://www.astro4dev.org/logic-model/.

11. Office of Astronomy for Development, Logic Model, Sahar Mohy-Ud-Din, OAD fellow. http://www.astro4dev.org/logic-model/.

12. Office of Astronomy for Development, Logic Model, Sahar Mohy-Ud-Din, OAD fellow. http://www.astro4dev.org/logic-model/.

13. Office of Astronomy for Development, Logic Model, Sahar Mohy-Ud-Din, OAD fellow. http://www.astro4dev.org/logic-model/.

14. Office of Astronomy for Development, Logic Model, Sahar Mohy-Ud-Din, OAD fellow. http://www.astro4dev.org/logic-model/.

15. Office of Astronomy for Development, Logic Model, Sahar Mohy-Ud-Din, OAD fellow. http://www.astro4dev.org/logic-model/.

16. W.K. Kellogg Foundation. 2004. Logic Model – Development Guide. http://www.wkkf.org/knowledge- center/resources/2006/02/WK-Kellogg-Foundation-Logic- ModelDevelopment-Guide.aspx.

17. McCawley, P.F. n.d. The Logic Model for Program Planning and Evaluation. https://www.cals.uidaho.edu/edcomm/pdf/CIS/CIS1097.pdf.

18. OECD. N.d. *Detailed Guide to Evaluating Financial Education Programmes.* https://www.oecd.org/finance/financial-education/49994090.pdf education/49994090.pdf.

READING LIST FOR HIGH-ACHIEVING WOMEN

Daniels, Marshawn Evans. *Believe Bigger, Discover the Path to your Life Purpose.* New York: Howard Evans Books, 2019.

Dweck, Carol. *Mindset: The New Psychology of Success.* New York: Ballantine and the House, LLC., 2006.

Evans, Gail. *Play Like a Man, Win Like a Woman.*, New York: Broadway Books, 2000.

George, Bill. *True North.* New Jersey: John Wiley & Sons, 2015.

Gladwell, Malcolm. *The Tipping Point: How Little Things Can Make A Big Difference.* Little Brown and Company, 2011.

Goldsmith, Marshall. *What Got You Here Won't Get You There.* New York: Hyperion, 2007.

Harris, Carla. *Strategize to Win. Penguin Putnam, Inc.*, 2014.

Johnson, Spencer, M.D. *Peaks and Valleys.* New York: Atria Books, 2009.

Kay, Kathy and Shipman, Claire. *The Confidence Code.* New York: HarperCollins Publishers, 2015.

Klaus, Peggy, *BRAG! The Art of Tooting Your Own Horn Without Blowing It.* New York: Warner Business Books, 2003.

Martineau, Jennifer, W., and Mount, Portia A. *Kick Some Glass.* New York: McGraw-Hill Education, 2018.

Obama, Michelle. *Becoming.* New York: Crown Publishing Group, 2018.

Wicker, Lisa J. Lindsay. *Power Play! Discovering the Secrets to Spirit-Winning Success.* Michigan: Victory House Press, 2001.

LEADERSHIP QUOTES FOR HIGH-ACHIEVING WOMEN

This is the true joy in life, being used for a purpose recognized by yourself as a mighty one. Being a force of nature instead of a feverish, selfish little clod of ailments and grievances, complaining that the world will not devote itself to making you happy. I am of the opinion that my life belongs to the whole community and as long as I live, it is my privilege to do for it what I can. I want to be thoroughly used up when I die, for the harder I work, the more I live. I rejoice in life for its own sake. Life is no brief candle to me. It is a sort of splendid torch which I have got hold of for the moment and I want to make it burn as brightly as possible before handing it on to future generations.

~George Bernard Shaw

If your actions create a legacy that inspires others to dream more, learn more, do more and become more, then, you are an excellent leader.

~Dolly Parton

Finally, I was able to see that if I had a contribution I wanted to make, I must do it, despite what others said. That I was OK the way I was. That it was all right to be strong.

~Wangari Maathai

Leadership is a series of behaviors rather than a role for heroes.
~Margaret Wheatley

The way to achieve your own success is to be willing to help somebody else get it first.

~Iyanla Vanzant

Champions keep playing until they get it right.
~Billie Jean King

Women belong in all places where decisions are being made. It shouldn't be that women are the exception.
~Ruth Bader Ginsburg

Life shrinks or expands in proportion to one's courage.
~Anais Nin

Many women live like it's a dress rehearsal. Ladies, the curtain is up and you're on.

~ Mikki Taylor

You're not in competition with other women. You're in competition with everyone.

~Tina Fey

Think like a queen. A queen is not afraid to fail. Failure is another stepping stone to greatness.
~Oprah Winfrey

There is a special place in hell for women who don't help other women.

~Madeleine Albright

Do not wait on a leader...look in the mirror, it's you!
~ *Katherine Miracle*

Leadership is about making others better as a result of your presence and making sure that impact lasts in your absence.
~*Sheryl Sandberg*

A woman is the full circle. Within her is the power to create, nurture and transform.
~*Diane Mariechil*

As women, we must stand up for ourselves. We must stand up for each other. We must stand up for justice for all.
~*Michelle Obama*

Also, by Dr. Lisa J. Lindsay Wicker

The Winning Spirit: Building Employee Enthusiasm
Power Play! Discover the Secret to Spirit-Winning Success
The Power Inside: Stretch (2-Disc)

Index

C

Capability 89
Capacity vii, viii, ix, x, xi, xiii, xvi,
    xvii, xx, xxiii, 3, 5, 7, 11, 22,
    24, 41, 69, 70, 72, 73, 75, 76,
    77, 79, 80, 81, 83, 85, 86, 88,
    92, 107, 109, 145, 146, 147
Capacity Altitude Pyramid 80, 81,
    88, 92
CAPA© Method 71
The CAPA© Method 71
Career vii, viii, ix, xi, xvii, xxi, 3, 5,
    6, 7, 9, 11, 12, 17, 18, 19, 21,
    22, 25, 27, 32, 38, 42, 53, 62,
    70, 71, 75, 76, 77, 81, 86, 87,
    89, 96, 98, 99, 102, 112, 126,
    145, 146, 148
Career Mastered xvii, 9, 19, 25, 27,
    62, 99, 102, 112, 146, 148
Career Mastered Magazine xvii, 9,
    25, 146
Career Mastered Women's
    Leadership Network 62, 99,
    112, 148
Challenges 5, 6, 24, 27, 41, 75, 126
Character 18, 61, 66
Chicago 121
Choice xv, xix, 3, 71, 72, 75, 76, 77
CJ Christopher 102
Claim vii, 8, 9, 10
Claim it 8, 9, 10
Clarity 40, 41
Clients 18, 25, 32, 42, 105, 108
Coherent 40
Commitment 50, 60, 61, 63, 64, 66,
    85, 92, 127
Committed 60, 61, 63, 64, 66, 100
Community xv, xvi, 75, 76, 101,
    109, 133, 145

Competition 32, 134
Confidence 12, 23, 131, 145
Conquer 12, 85, 86, 88, 89, 96
Consistent 8, 9, 10, 50, 51, 52, 53,
    55, 58, 61
Consulting Practice 18, 71
Conversion 116
Convert 23, 93, 98, 105, 107,
    110, 116
Corporate America 6, 75, 77,
    105, 145
COVID-19 6, 61, 125
Create 7, 8, 10, 11, 12, 13, 17, 18,
    19, 23, 38, 40, 41, 51, 52, 71,
    72, 81, 90, 99, 104, 105, 112,
    133, 135
C-Suite 6

D

Daily Schedule 55
Dance 8, 63
David vii, xvi, 70
Decision 21, 72, 83, 109, 122, 134
Degree 3, 50, 87, 98, 105, 121
Destiny 17, 103
Discipline 51, 52, 73
Discrimination 5, 99
Distractions 54, 90

E

Elephant 41, 42, 44, 48, 93, 108
Embrace 19, 38, 40, 54, 55
End 4, 12, 43, 60, 62, 76, 85, 87, 88,
    92, 104, 116
Enthusiast 81
Environment 4, 5, 19, 76, 110
Evaluation 108, 129, 130
Excel Village xvii, 112
Exercise xi, 11, 63

U

Ultimate Impact 108, 109
United Nations 128, 129

V

Value xv, 17, 18, 19, 23, 24, 38, 41,
    42, 43, 50, 53, 72, 81, 100,
    105, 107, 108, 148
Value Proposition 19, 24
Victory 132
Vilfredo Pareto 42
Visualize 79, 90, 92

W

Walk 7, 8, 10, 12, 51, 75, 76, 93,
    96, 100
Winning 7, 101, 112, 132, 136
Women vii, viii, ix, x, xi, xiii, xvi,
    xx, xxi, 3, 4, 5, 6, 7, 9, 11, 17,
    18, 19, 20, 27, 42, 61, 62, 63,
    66, 71, 77, 81, 86, 87, 96, 98,
    99, 100, 101, 102, 103, 104,
    105, 109, 112, 125, 127, 128,
    129, 131, 133, 134, 135, 145,
    146, 147, 148

A SPECIAL OFFERING
Introduce *Capacity: Women Shattering The Limits — Now!* to your organization

Dr. Lisa J. Lindsay Wicker is to career development what the Fairy Godmother is to Cinderella. She is key cast member who embodies hope, access, wisdom and encouragement to participate in your success.

With her exposure to leaders within business communities across corporate America and beyond our borders, she has inspired women to gain the confidence to climb the ladder where many find themselves stuck.

In Capacity: Women Shattering The Limits — Now! Dr. Wicker encourages women to take back their power, give themselves permission to win, develop their voice, be true to themselves, and get clear about their career vision. She provides a strategy for women to win by using their Capacity to break free and shatter any limits to design the career and life desired.

Benefit from Dr. Wicker's wisdom and years of leadership experience with the following opportunities for your organization:

Bestselling author of *The Winning Spirit* and Founder of *Career Mastered*

DR. LISA LINDSAY WICKER

CAPACITY

WOMEN SHATTERING THE LIMITS - NOW!

Foreword by *Florine Mark*, President and CEO of The WW (Weight Watchers) Group, Inc.

Special Keynote Address for your organization on Capacity & Leadership. A candid presentation on how to use your capacity and leadership to move your career forward, now. Every audience member will receive a copy of *Capacity: Women Shattering The Limits — Now!* and an online subscription to the *Career Mastered* magazine, a quarterly women's leadership advancement publication.

Shatter the Limits Masterclass with Dr. Lisa Lindsay Wicker. A six-week virtual online class. Participants will have access to the class library and videos and will receive a copy of *Capacity: Women Shattering The Limits — Now!*

Corporate membership with the Career Mastered Women's Leadership Network exists to provide diverse opportunities for corporations to invest in programs that have a global outreach to acknowledge, support, award and celebrate women and girls.

Through our Corporate Diversity in Excellence program, we offer various ways for corporations to invest and support female global leaders' historical and phenomenal impact.

Contact Dr. Wicker to bring her compelling message to your organization or become a Corporate partner to benefit your women leaders.

Linwick & Associates, LLC.
Creating Organizational Value Through People
www.drlisawicker.com, www.careermastered.com, www.lwaco.com